PENGUIN

APHORISMS

Georg Christoph Lichtenberg was born in 1742 in Oberramstadt, Germany, the youngest of seventeen children. From early youth he suffered from a malformation of the spine. In 1763 he joined the University of Göttingen, where he studied mathematics and the natural sciences and, in 1770, was appointed a professor at the university. In the same year he briefly went to England. This was followed by a second visit during 1774–5; after his return to Göttingen he became notorious for his anglophilia and as an advocate of almost everything English. He was highly regarded in academic life and a popular lecturer. As well as his scientific writings he wrote *Letters from England* (1776 and 1778) and a book on Hogarth. Lichtenberg died in 1799.

R. J. Hollingdale was born in London in 1930. Among his many translations are Nietzsche's *Thus Spoke Zarathustra*, *Ecce Homo*, *Twilight of the Idols*, *The Anti-Christ* and *Beyond Good and Evil*, *A Nietzsche Reader*, Goethe's *Elective Affinities*, Schopenhauer's *Essays and Aphorisms* and a selection of Hoffmann's *Tales* for Penguin Classics.

GEORG CHRISTOPH LICHTENBERG

APHORISMS

Translated with an Introduction and Notes by
R. J. Hollingdale

PENGUIN BOOKS

PENGUIN BOOKS

Published by the Penguin Group
27 Wrights Lane, London W8 5TZ, England
Viking Penguin Inc., 40 West 23rd Street, New York, New York 10010, USA
Penguin Books Australia Ltd, Ringwood, Victoria, Australia
Penguin Books Canada Ltd, 2801 John Street, Markham, Ontario, Canada L3R 1B4
Penguin Books (NZ) Ltd, 182–190 Wairau Road, Auckland 10, New Zealand

Penguin Books Ltd, Registered Offices: Harmondsworth, Middlesex, England

First published 1990
1 3 5 7 9 10 8 6 4 2

Translation, Introduction and Notes copyright © R. J. Hollingdale, 1990
All rights reserved

Made and printed in Great Britain by
Cox and Wyman Ltd, Reading, Berks
Filmset in Linotron Ehrhardt by
Rowland Phototypesetting Ltd, Bury St Edmunds, Suffolk

CONTENTS

INTRODUCTION

I

The body of this book consists of 1,085 aphorisms and other aphoristically brief writings selected from the notebooks Lichtenberg kept from his student days until the end of his life as a depository for his thoughts, observations and memoranda to himself. He called these volumes his '*Sudelbücher*' – a rendition of the English 'wastebooks', a term employed in the English business house of the time to designate the ledgers in which transactions of all kinds were entered as they occurred before being transferred to the more orderly and neatly written account books. Each volume was accorded a letter of the alphabet (with I omitted) from A, begun in 1765 (and in fact consisting of five slim notebooks collected together), to L, which breaks off at Lichtenberg's death in 1799. Notebooks G and H existed into the nineteenth century but have since disappeared, most of notebook K was at some time destroyed, and notebook L has a number of pages missing.

The contents of these notebooks are very heterogeneous: a single page can include aphorisms, scientific jottings and sketches, linguistic experiments, phrases that have struck the writer and appealed to him, quotations from books and magazines, notes for future work, dates to be remembered, titles of books to be purchased; what the *Sudelbücher* are not, however, are diaries – Lichtenberg also kept diaries and the orderly descriptions of the day-to-day events of his life they contain bear no resemblance to the pages of the notebooks.

The contents of our volume first appeared in print in the first and second editions of *Lichtenbergs Vermischte Schriften* (1800–1806 and 1844–53); in making my selection I used the text of volumes 1 and 2 of Wolfgang Promies's edition of Lichtenberg's *Schriften und Briefe* (1968–71), in which the lost notebooks G and H and the missing pages of notebook K are reconstructed, as far as this is possible, from the texts published in volumes of the *Vermischte Schriften* of 1806 and 1844. An additional notebook, called by Promies the '*Goldpapierheft*' from the colour of its original binding, has also been drawn on for the present edition; and I found Wilhelm Grenzmann's selection in his edition of the *Gesammelte Werke* (1949) useful in determining what I thought to be the best of Lichtenberg.

2

Lichtenberg is credited with having introduced the aphorism into German literature, but he did so posthumously and without deliberate intent: he published much during his lifetime but the notebooks in which he wrote his aphorisms were kept entirely for his own use, instruction and amusement, with no thought of publication. He was a mathematician, physicist and astronomer by profession, and a satirist in his spare time: but the work he published would not have served to keep his name and presence alive beyond his own era. His scientific writings belong firmly to their age; of his non-scientific works the *Letters from England* (1776 and 1778) are remembered chiefly for their descriptions of Garrick, and his book on Hogarth – *G. C. Lichtenbergs ausführliche Erklärung der Hogarthischen Kupferstiche* (1794–9) – survives in literary history as an amazing *tour de force* or an amazing act of folly, depending on how you look at it (the descriptions and explanations of Hogarth's drawings are so detailed as to render the drawings themselves almost redundant); and probably none of them would have outlasted him even to the qualified degree they have if they had not been by the author of the aphorisms.

As a distinct literary form the aphorism was, like so many things good and bad, an invention of antique Greece. The word itself is first encountered at the head of the so-called *Corpus Hippocraticum*: the collection of treatises, of which more than seventy are known, named after Hippocrates, the 'father of medicine', and consisting of rules for good living and good health, brief reflections and other short writings of a kind which, from the description accorded them, we should now call aphoristic. The epigram and the 'sentence' or proverb are plainly related to the aphorism, the character of the Romans and their language is equally plainly favourable to aphoristic brevity, and all good writers have tended towards aphorism when they have wanted to summarize an opinion: none the less the aphorism as a deliberately cultivated literary form, as distinct from something said briefly, did not appear in European literature until the Renaissance, when the aphoristic writings of Erasmus, Michelangelo, Paracelsus and Bacon, but above all those of the line of French philosophers from Montaigne to Chamfort, bestowed on it the distinctive character by which we now recognize it.

In its pure and perfect form the aphorism is distinguished by four qualities occurring together: it is brief, it is isolated, it is witty, and it is 'philosophical'. This last quality marks it off from the epigram, which is essentially no more than a witty observation; the third, which it shares with the epigram, marks it off from the proverb or maxim: its point, though intended seriously, is supposed to strike the reader, not with the blunt obviousness of a palpable truth – 'Many hands make light work' – but rather in the way the point of a good joke should strike him – 'In the misfortunes of our best friends we find something that does not displease us.' In this pure form the aphorism disdains all giving of reasons and presents only a conclusion, so that it is often plainly intended to provoke instant contradiction in the sense that the pay-off line of a joke is intended to provoke instant laughter.

That Lichtenberg was a master of the aphorism in its pure form is amply demonstrated in the following selection. 'To err is *human* also in so far as animals seldom or never err, or at least only the cleverest of them do so', to take one example, seems to me as perfect a model of the form as can be found anywhere: the cliché that, in contrast to the infallibility of God, error is the province of humanity, is reinterpreted to contrast humanity unfavourably with the animals in this respect, then the basis of this judgement is disclosed in the 'shock' substitution of 'cleverest' for the expected 'stupidest'. The meaning of the aphorism is: if God is infallible, so also is animal instinct (or almost so), and error is introduced only when human or near-human reason begins to operate. The purpose of clothing this observation in aphoristic form is to compel the reader to make it for himself and thus, through the effect of vanity and a feeling of proprietorship, be more inclined to accept it as true.

The close association between the aphorism and the joke was something Lichtenberg himself was aware of – or so it seems from his observation that the 'inventor' of knowledge is 'wit', while reason is only its 'discoverer'; and the connection is still quite close even when the aphorism has expanded into a miniature essay of several sentences: the linking together of things we do not normally link together, and some feeling of a punch-line at the end, are still its defining characteristics.

3

The isolation to which the aphorism consigns itself often has to be paid for in imperfect comprehensibility: its reader must often possess a background of knowledge against which alone it will acquire comprehensive meaning. This is so, for instance, even in the case of the aphorism of La Rochefoucauld quoted earlier: if it is to be seen as having any *raison d'être* at all we must at the very least be aware that common sentiment is opposed to it. This is why the need has often been felt to understand Lichtenberg's aphorisms as the salient points of a deep philosophical front – of a body of thought, that is, which if its author had been differently disposed could have been expressed differently. During the nineteenth century this need was reinforced in those who admired Lichtenberg by the hegemony of the philosophical system: if a philosopher did not have a system, it was felt, he was not really a philosopher. In the present century the fragmentary philosophy of Nietzsche's notebooks and of the later Wittgenstein has encouraged the suspicion that Lichtenberg's fragmentary philosophy is of a kind similar to that of Nietzsche or Wittgenstein. For my part I think that anyone who conscientiously seeks 'Lichtenberg's philosophy' in the *Sudelbücher* is not exactly wasting his time – no one who reads Lichtenberg conscientiously is wasting his time – but is certainly expending ingenuity in the wrong place: the analogy with Nietzsche or Wittgenstein is misleading, in as much as their thinking is only expressed in fragmentary form whereas Lichtenberg's really is fragmentary. His notebooks resemble little else in literature for variegated inconsequentiality, and even when the aphoristic and allied writings have been extracted and tidied up – punctuation, for example, is often noticeable by its complete absence – the degree of cohesion they exhibit derives, not from any submerged systematism, or even from a personal philosophy struggling to find expression, but simply from their being the product of the same mind and from that mind's being infused with what we have come to call the 'spirit of the Enlightenment'.

The reader may recall Nietzsche's remark, in the preface to the *Genealogy of Morals*, that the 'aphoristic form' of *Thus Spoke*

Zarathustra 'creates difficulty' for those who want to understand it: this difficulty, he says, 'arises from the fact that today this form is not taken *sufficiently seriously*. An aphorism, properly stamped and moulded, has not been "deciphered" when it has simply been read; one has then rather to begin its *exegesis*, for which is required an art of exegesis.' There is no evidence that Lichtenberg thought of *his* 'aphorisms' in this serious and solemn way. Not only were they not 'properly stamped and moulded', but he in fact never employed the word aphorism to describe what he wrote: the earliest edition of his aphoristic writings entitles them '*Bemerkungen vermischten Inhalts*' ('Remarks on Various Subjects') and the word aphorism was first used prominently by Albert Leitzmann as the title of his edition of 1902 and succeeding years. What Lichtenberg himself calls them, in an expression very characteristic of him, is '*Pfennigs-Wahrheiten*' – 'truths in pennyworths'. If these pennyworths in any way add up to a pound it is only because Lichtenberg is a singularly pure instance of the spirit of the Enlightenment operating upon what it has inherited.

This inheritance was for Lichtenberg his native German Pietist tradition as it had been modified by the effects of the French and English Enlightenment and by the most influential philosophers of his day, Leibniz and Kant. Like so many who have contributed to the humane culture of Germany, he was a son of the manse: his father and both grandfathers were Lutheran clergymen, and his paternal grandfather, a contemporary of Spener, the founder of Pietism, fell strongly under Spener's influence and became a Pietist. The movement was extremely influential throughout Germany from the middle of the seventeenth century onwards, but, unlike similar non-conformist movements in Britain and elsewhere, it did not involve its adherents in a breach with the established church or the setting up of new 'non-conformist' churches. From the point of view of understanding Lichtenberg's background, two characteristics of the Pietist faith need to be noticed.

The first has to do with its power to preserve belief in the existence of God well beyond a loss of belief in the veracity of any existing church. The Catholic proposition with regard to Protestantism that, constituting as it does a breach with the one true faith as revealed to and transmitted by the one true church, it is only a stage on the road to atheism may in the long run be proved true (it is too soon to tell);

but in the short term it has proved the reverse of the truth. The so-called deism of the French *philosophes*, succeeded by the frank atheism of the period of the Revolution, was an outcome of the absolutist mentality of Catholic France: either the Christian God as preached by the one true church, or no or next-to-no God at all. In Protestant Germany, on the contrary, the believer was presented with no such either–or demand. The existence of the Lutheran church was in itself a demonstration that to deny the church of Rome in no way involved a denial of God; this being so, the non-conformist who took the further step of denying the Lutheran church, at least as far as inward conviction was concerned, could do so in the confident expectation that God would still be with him; and the same was true if the non-conformist took the yet further step of denying all organized religion, and indeed all distinctly Christian belief of any kind – he still felt under no constraint at the same time to abandon belief in God. So it was that in Germany the age of the Enlightenment was not at the same time an age of atheism or near-atheism, and that the first German philosopher who was also an atheist was Schopenhauer (*The World as Will and Idea*, 1818). Lichtenberg tells us that he ceased to be a believing Christian at the age of sixteen, but his notebooks make it clear that this loss of faith did not involve him in a loss of belief in the supernatural altogether: that God exists he seems never to doubt, though he is quite sure that the fact cannot be proved. This does indeed look like a halfway stage to atheism – the Catholic position is, of course, that the existence of God *can* be proved, though it is also known to us through revelation – but to Lichtenberg himself it was hardly more than a move in the direction in which the Pietist tradition would naturally have taken him.

The second characteristic is that German Pietism was capable of a high degree of secularization. Although the Pietists were for a long period content to be known as the *Stillen im Lande* – 'quietists' who left the affairs of the world in the hands of others – the movement also inspired the evolution of a social conscience more in accord with Spener's original conception: for to Spener the individual's moral self-improvement was not far removed from vanity if it was not accompanied by the performance of Christian good works. Pietists, and the much more numerous host of those whose conscience had been Pietized without their knowing it, thus came to equate effecting social improvements with doing the work of the Lord (a species of do-goodism, if you like, provided you are willing to think of Bismarck as a do-gooder). That this is the highway to the secularization of religion hardly needs pointing out; what may not be so clear is that it will certainly have running along beside it a parallel highway to the secularization of thinking. The distance in time between P. J. Spener (1635–1705) and G. C. Lichtenberg (1742–99) is not very great, but mentally they inhabit different ages: Spener thinks, and cannot help thinking, as a theologian; Lichtenberg regards theology as being, like everything else, subject to the judgement of the philosopher, who has unseated the theologian as the supreme arbiter in the realm of speculative thought. In differing in this way Spener and Lichtenberg are entirely representative of their respective epochs: for, in Germany at least, philosophy is theology secularized.

Lichtenberg entered philosophy as a distinct discipline through the philosophy of Leibniz, for which the fundamental optimism of the Pietist faith made him especially receptive. As the final and supreme exponent of philosophical rationalism Leibniz appealed strongly to an age in which instinctive certitude as to the nature of the metaphysical world was on the wane. He seemed to prove, as though by mathematics (this is the essence of the appeal of philosophical rationalism), that the world was a structure all of whose parts are in harmony with one another, that there were no 'gaps' in this structure within which chance (i.e. evil) might operate but that the law of causality was effective everywhere, and that all had been forethought and fore-arranged by an omnipotent and benevolent God – in short, that this is the best of all possible worlds, a proposition one was in danger of calling into question. Something of Leibniz remained with Lichtenberg to the end; he never lost his belief, for instance, that the world was a harmonious whole; but his belief in Leibniz as a whole could not survive his two visits to England, where the scepticism of the Enlightenment and the empiricism of contemporary British philosophy combined to undermine the credibility not only of Leibniz but of any comprehensive metaphysical system whatever. The change he underwent is well expressed in his saying that he now dealt in truths in pennyworths – an undertaking which might be called the opposite of the wholesale trading practised by the rationalist systems of continental Europe. He became an empiricist and a sceptic, and so he remained until his thinking received its final redirection from Kant. Much has been written about Lichtenberg's relationship with Kant, the general drift of which has been that he failed to understand him; Grenzmann even goes so far as to say that at bottom he got nothing out of him at all. A true perspective can perhaps be obtained if we regard him as having been too close to Kant (1724–1804) to be able to see him entire. What emerges unequivocally from his notebooks is that Kant offered him a corrective to the exclusively objective orientation encouraged by empiricist philosophy by directing him back to the subjective apparatus by means of which cognition of any kind is performed: to speculation about the objective world he added speculation about objectivity itself.

4

Lichtenberg was born on 1 July 1742 in Oberramstadt, near Darmstadt, as the youngest of the seventeen children of the pastor of Oberramstadt most of whom had died at birth or in infancy. From early youth he suffered from a malformation of the spine, the precise origin of which is unknown, which developed into a hump. That Lichtenberg was a hunchback was a fact that coloured his whole life and is one that has to be remembered and taken into account when we read what he writes about himself.

His native intelligence was, it seems, evident from the first, and his disinclination to follow his family into the church made an academic career an obvious choice for him. In 1763 a stipend granted him by the local landgrave enabled him to attend the university at Göttingen, where he studied mathematics and the natural sciences and around which his life thereafter revolved: in 1770 he was appointed an extraordinary professor, in 1775 a professor in ordinary, which he remained until his death. He taught mathematics, physics, astronomy and a variety of other more or less scientific subjects.

Before his appointment but after his studies had been officially concluded he stayed on in Göttingen as tutor to a number of English aristocratic youths whose fathers had sent them to Germany as a way of broadening, if not their minds, then at any rate their experience, and he produced upon them so favourable an impression that, their studies (whatever they might have been) over, they insisted he be invited to England both for his own sake and for the sake of those who would be fortunate enough to meet him. As a consequence Lichtenberg paid two visits to England – from Easter to early summer 1770 and from August 1774 to Christmas 1775 – and their importance for him and for the course of his thinking cannot be exaggerated. London was by far the largest, grandest and most stimulating thing he had ever seen, and he remarks again and again on its colossal size, wealth, variety and vitality (though before taking what he says completely at face value we must call to mind that he was all the time unconsciously contrasting London with Darmstadt and Göttingen). He was welcomed into the highest society as well as into the most learned: George III and Queen Charlotte, who could of course both speak German, took great pleasure in his conversation, and one morning the king caused enormous consternation at his lodgings by coming there unannounced for a private discussion (according to reports he arrived on the doorstep at 10 a.m. and when the door was opened to his knock asked in German whether the Herr Professor was at home). He visited everywhere he could think of visiting, most memorably Drury Lane, where Garrick was in the last year of his career. Outside London he visited Bath, Birmingham (Matthew Boulton's factory, the world's first assembly line), and Margate, England's oldest public bathing resort, a phenomenon then unknown in Germany. After his return to Göttingen at the end of 1775 he became notorious for his anglophilia and as an advocate of almost everything English – when Kotzebue wrote an abusive satire on his private life he included the phrase 'I clothed her with British generosity' so that the object of his attack should not remain in doubt.

Embarked on his academic career in earnest, Lichtenberg quite soon acquired celebrity not only for his erudition but even more for the engaging and entertaining way in which he imparted it: he enjoyed a genuine popularity, and many of those who composed his overflowing audiences came not to learn but to 'hear Lichtenberg'. He was among the first to introduce experiments with apparatus into his lectures, and over the years he assembled a fine collection of the scientific apparatus of his day, especially that which produced or was otherwise involved with electricity. In 1780, to the great alarm of his neighbours, he erected the first lightning-conductor ever seen in Göttingen (lightning-conductors were supposed to be dangerous, and some of them were: it was not always understood that they had to be firmly earthed). He had already produced experimentally the phenomena known thereafter as the 'Lichtenberg figures' (star-shaped patterns formed by dust or other fine matter settling on the surface of an inductor), and he had tried to snatch electricity from the air by means of kites. In 1784 Alessandro Volta, the father of the volt, visited Göttingen especially to see Lichtenberg and his electrical equipment.

His scientific writings show him to have been informed about the then frontiers of scientific progress, but it was not given him to make any practical scientific discovery, a fact he attributed in part to an unconquerable tendency to procrastination (which may, in fact, be the explanation of his failure to launch the first hydrogen-filled balloon, for he certainly knew how to do it well before the famous ascent from the Champs de Mars in August 1783). None the less he was in 1793 elected a member of the Royal Society.

His private life was very irregular, though not very much more so than that of several even more celebrated Germans of his age. In 1777 he met Maria Stechard, then aged thirteen and 'a model of beauty and sweetness', who thereafter visited him every day and from Easter 1780 lived with him permanently. His relationship with his 'little daughter' was well known in Göttingen, but nobody was really bothered by it and only the dramatist Kotzebue saw fit to 'expose' Lichtenberg's mode of life in a satirical pamphlet of an incomprehensible aggressiveness. Maria died in August 1782 and Lichtenberg was affected by her death as by nothing before or afterwards. During the following year, however, he encountered another woman of the people, the 22-year-old Margarethe Kellner, and from 1786 onwards they lived together. Margarethe gave Lichtenberg six children; they were married in October 1789, and she survived him by forty-nine years.

5

On 10 August 1846 the dramatist Friedrich Hebbel wrote in his diary the subsequently much-quoted remark: 'I would rather be forgotten with Lichtenberg than immortal with Jean Paul.' The remark is calculated to bring a smile to the face of the reader nowadays, for Jean Paul's immortality was cut short rather quickly, while Lichtenberg is the best-remembered representative in Germany of the age of the

Enlightenment. During the almost two centuries since his death on 24 February 1799 he has come close to being the German writer's favourite writer. Goethe commended him as being worthy of study 'in a way that few are'; Schopenhauer singled him out as an example of the true philosopher who thinks not for the instruction of others but because 'thinking for himself' is his greatest pleasure; Nietzsche counted his aphorisms as one of the only four German books which, apart from Goethe's, were worth reading again and again; in the 1920s Kurt Tucholsky regretted the unavailability of his writings ('*Wo ist Lichtenberg?*'). In his book on *The Germans* (1982), Gordon A. Craig describes Lichtenberg's aphorisms as being 'among the great achievements of the German spirit in the eighteenth century'; Lichtenberg himself he calls 'a formidable critic who directed his shafts against charlatans, mystagogues and purveyors of false science' and 'an inveterate opponent of provincial patriotism, that "*Teutschheit*" which was really a disguised form of xenophobia' whose 'brilliant sallies against this recurrent German disease were to win the praise of people like Heinrich Heine, Leo Tolstoy, Karl Kraus and Albert Einstein, all of them spiritual heirs of the Enlightenment'. This formidable array of recommendations, which would presumably have greatly astonished Lichtenberg himself if he could have known of it, may suggest that the general unfamiliarity of his name and writings that exists outside Germany is something to be remedied.

This selection from Lichtenberg is ordered chronologically, from notebook A to notebook L: this seems to me in every way preferable to trying (and failing) to arrange each aphorism under a subject heading appropriate to it. It also serves to preserve something of what is in fact before us in the original, which is not an orderly series of prescriptions and commandments but a very disorderly series of notebook jottings extending over thirty years. The attentive reader will notice that one or two aphorisms appear more than once, in slightly different wording; and he will also understand why they do.

An asterisk at the end of a numbered section indicates that there is a note on that section at the end of the book. I have kept these annotations as brief and as few as I could: to annotate an aphorism seems to me too much like explaining a joke. Generally I have worked on a need-to-know basis: does the reader need to know this in order to understand the aphorism? Assuming that the reader already knows who, for instance, Plato or Montaigne or Captain Cook are, and does not need to know who, for instance, Banks (D 23) or Dr Price (D 102) are, I found that what needed annotating was chiefly details of Lichtenberg's life, a number of less familiar German writers referred to, a few linguistic points, and a few references to contemporary events.

February 1988   R. J. H.

FROM LICHTENBERG'S NOTEBOOKS

1765–1770

1

The great artifice of regarding small deviations from the truth as being the truth itself is at the same time the foundation of wit, where the whole thing would often collapse if we were to regard these deviations in a spirit of philosophical rigour.

2

It is a question whether in the arts and sciences a *best* is possible beyond which our understanding cannot go. Perhaps this point is infinitely distant, notwithstanding that with every closer approximation we have less in front of us.

3

With many a science the endeavour to discover a universal principle is perhaps often just as fruitless as would be the endeavour of a mineralogist to discover a primal universal substance out of which all the minerals had arisen. Nature creates, not *genera* and *species*, but *individua*, and our shortsightedness has to seek out similarities so as to be able to retain in mind many things at the same time. These conceptions become more and more inaccurate the larger the families we invent for ourselves are.

4

The greatest things in the world are brought about by other things which we count as nothing: little causes we overlook but which at length accumulate.

5

Rousseau was right to call accent the soul of speech, and we often regard people as stupid and when we look into it we find it is merely the simple sound of their manner of speaking.

6

To fit the metre to the thought is a very difficult art and one the neglect of which is in large part responsible for the ludicrous in verse. Metre and thought are related to one another as, in ordinary life, life-style is to office.

7

If we want to draw up a philosophy that will be useful to us in life, or if we want to offer universal rules for a perpetually contented life, then, to be sure, we have to abstract from that which introduces a much too great diversity into our contemplations – somewhat as we often do in mathematics when we forget friction and other similar particular properties of bodies so that the calculation will not be too difficult for us, or at least replace such properties with a single letter. Small misfortunes incontestably introduce a large measure of uncertainty into these practical rules, so that we have to dismiss them from our mind and turn our attention only to overcoming the greater misfortunes. This is incontestably the true meaning of certain propositions of the Stoic philosophy.

8

Superstition originates among ordinary people in the early and all too zealous instruction they receive in religion: they hear of mysteries, miracles, deeds of the Devil, and consider it very probable that things of this sort could occur in everything anywhere. If, on the other hand, they were first taught about nature itself, they would more readily regard the supernatural and mysterious elements of religion with greater awe, instead of considering them as something extremely commonplace, as they do now – so commonplace, indeed, that they think it nothing out of the ordinary if someone tells them six angels walked down the street today . . .

9

There are no such things as synonyms: the inventors of the words we regard as synonyms certainly expressed in them not one thing but presumably species.

10

One might call habit a moral friction: something that prevents the mind from gliding over things but connects it with them and makes it hard for it to free itself from them.

11

At least once a week a dietetic sermon should be preached in church, and if our clergy too would acquire this science spiritual reflections could be woven into it that are here very apposite; for it is hardly to be believed how spiritual reflections when mixed with a little physics can hold people's attention and give them a livelier idea of God than do the often ill-applied examples of his wrath.

12

The fear of death which is imprinted in men is at the same time a great expedient Heaven employs to hinder them from many misdeeds: many things are left undone for fear of imperilling one's life or health.

13

The proof that there is a future life advanced by philosophers, which consists in saying that God could not reward our last moments if there were not, belongs among the proofs by analogy: we always reward after the act, consequently God also does so. But we do so when we cannot see ahead; when we are not prevented by this disability we also reward in advance. We pay an advance subscription to a university, for instance: may God too not have paid an advance subscription? . . .

14

Food probably has a very great influence on the condition of men. Wine exercises a more visible influence, food does it more slowly but perhaps just as surely. Who knows if a well-prepared soup was not responsible for the pneumatic pump or a poor one for a war?

15

I have seen that fervent ambition and mistrustfulness always go together.

16

When sometimes I had drunk a lot of coffee, and was consequently startled by anything, I noticed quite distinctly that I was startled before I heard the noise: we thus hear as it were with other organs as well as with our ears.

17

Prejudices are so to speak the mechanical instincts of men: through their prejudices they do without any effort many things they would find too difficult to think through to the point of resolving to do them.

18

We must take care that in seeking to demonstrate the possibility of many things we do not all too quickly appeal to the power of an all-perfect being: for as soon as one believes, e.g., that God makes matter think one can no longer demonstrate that a god exists apart from matter.

19

Our life is so precisely balanced between pleasure and pain that things that serve to maintain us can sometimes cause us harm, as for instance a quite natural change in the air. But who knows whether much of our pleasure does not depend on this balance; perhaps our sensitivity in this matter is an important part of that which constitutes our superiority over the animals.

20

A sensation expressed in words is like music described in words: the expressions we use are not sufficiently at one with the thing to be expressed. The poet who wants to excite sympathy directs the reader to a painting, and through this to the thing to be expressed. A painted landscape gives instant delight, but one celebrated in verse has first to be painted in the reader's own head . . .

21

In order to become really sensible of a piece of good fortune which seems to us a matter of indifference we must imagine we had lost it and have recovered it again at just this moment; to undertake this experiment successfully, however, requires a certain amount of experience in all sorts of suffering.

22

The excuses we make to ourselves when we want to do something are excellent material for soliloquies, for they are rarely made except when we are alone, and are very often made aloud.

23

In his *Comedy*, Dante Alighieri names Virgil, with many tokens of respect, as his teacher, and yet, as Herr Meinhard remarks, makes such ill use of him: a clear proof that even in the days of Dante one praised the ancients without knowing why. This respect for poets one does not understand and yet wishes to equal is the source of the bad writing in our literature.

24

To understand the true meaning of a word of our mother tongue certainly often takes us many years. By understanding I also include the meanings that can be bestowed upon it by the way in which it is spoken. The signification of a word is – to express myself mathematically – given us in a formula in which the way it is spoken is the variable and the word itself the constant quantity. Here there opens up a way of endlessly enriching the languages without increasing the number of words. I have found that we enunciate the phrase *Es ist gut* in five different ways and each time with a different meaning, which is, to be sure, often also determined by a third variable quantity, namely facial expression.

25

The *animalcula infusoria* are bladders with desires.

26

It is we who are the measure of what is strange and miraculous: if we sought a universal measure the strange and miraculous would not occur and all things would be equal.

27

Minds detached from an external world must be strange creatures; for, since the ground of every thought lies in the mind, such minds would be capable of the strangest combinations of ideas. We call people mad when the regulation of their conceptions no longer corresponds to the sequence of events in our regular world; for which reason a careful observation of nature, or of mathematics, is certainly the most effective specific against madness; nature is, so to speak, the guide-rope by which our thoughts are led so that they shall not wander away.

28

The grocer who weighs something is as much engaged in putting the unknown quantity on one side and the known on the other as is the algebraist.

29

The contention over *signification* and *being* which has caused such mischief in religion would perhaps have been more salutary if it had been conducted in respect to other subjects, for it is a general source of misfortune to us that we believe things are in actuality what they in fact only signify.

30

It is a wholly unavoidable fault of all languages that they express only the *genera* of concepts and seldom say adequately what they intend to say. For if we compare our words with things we shall find that the latter proceed in a quite different series from the former. The qualities we perceive in our souls are connected in such a way it is not at all easy to assign a boundary between any two of them; this is not so in the case of the words with which we express them, and two consecutive and related qualities are expressed by signs which seem to us to have no relationship with one another. We should be able to decline words philosophically, that is to indicate their relationship through modifications. In mathematical analysis, the undetermined part of a line a we call x, and the remainder we call, not y as in ordinary life, but $a-x$. That is why mathematical language possesses such a great advantage over ordinary language.

31

No prince will ever define the merit of a man by conferring favours, since numerous examples have shown that rulers are not generally good men. The French king bakes pastries and ruins honest girls. The King of Spain carves up hares to the sound of drum-rolls and fanfares. The last King of Poland who was Elector of Saxony peppered his court jester's arse with shot. The Prince of Löwenstein, when a great fire had devastated his property, bewailed only the loss of his saddle. To please a dancer, the Landgrave of Kassel rode his horse into the suite of another prince who is no better either: he is deceived by the most miserable of creatures. The Duke of Württemberg is crazy. The King of England put a bun in Miss P.'s oven. The Prince of Weilburg bathed publicly in the river Lahn . . . And these are the greatest among men. How, then, can we expect human affairs to proceed in a tolerable fashion? Of what use are introductions into the art of commercial management if the overlord of the whole is some buffoon who acknowledges no sovereignty but that of his own stupidity, caprice, whores and valets? Oh, if only the world would wake up! If only three million of them were dangling on the gallows, perhaps fifty to eighty million others would be happy!

32

When Plato says the passions and natural desires are the wings of the soul he expresses himself in a very instructive way: such comparisons illuminate the subject and are as it were the translation of difficult concepts into a language familiar to everyone – true definitions.

33

The world is a body common to all men, changes to it bring about a change in the souls of all men who are turned towards that part of it at that moment.

34

Even at school I harboured ideas of suicide which were diametrically opposed to those commonly accepted in the world, and I recall that I once disputed in Latin in favour of suicide and sought to defend it . . . In August 1769 and in the following months I thought about suicide more than ever before, and I have at all times considered that a man in whom the instinct for self-preservation has become so weakened that it can so easily be overpowered may kill himself without incurring guilt. If a sin has been committed, it was committed a long time before . . .

35

The peasant who believes the moon is no bigger than a plough wheel never reflects that at a distance of a few miles a whole church appears only as a white speck but the moon on the contrary seems always to be the same size: what prevents him from connecting these ideas, which are all presented to him distinctly? In his ordinary life he does in fact connect ideas and perhaps does so by more artificial connections than these. This reflection should make the philosopher pay heed: perhaps in some of the connections he makes he is still a peasant. We think early in life but we do not know we are thinking, any more than we know we are growing or digesting; many ordinary people never do discover it. Close observation of external things easily leads back to the point of observation, ourselves, and conversely he who is for once wholly aware of himself easily proceeds from that to observing the things around him. Be attentive, feel nothing in vain, measure and compare: this is the whole law of philosophy.

36

It thunders, *howls*, *roars*, hisses, whistles, blusters, hums, growls, rumbles, *squeaks*, *groans*, *sings*, crackles, cracks, rattles, flickers, clicks, *snarls*, tumbles, *whimpers*, *whines*, rustles, *murmurs*, crashes, *clucks*, *to gurgle*, tinkles, *blows*, *snores*, claps, *to lisp*, *to cough*, it boils, to scream, to weep, to sob, to croak, to stutter, to lisp, to coo, to breathe, to clash, to bleat, to neigh, to grumble, to scrape, to bubble. These words, and others like them, which express sounds, are more than mere symbols: they are a kind of hieroglyphics for the ear.

37

The philosophy of mankind as such is the philosophy of one certain individual man corrected by the philosophy of others, even of fools, and this in accordance with the rules of a rational assessment of degrees of probability. Propositions on which all men are in agreement are true: if they are not true we have no truth at all.

38

To grow wiser means to learn to know better and better the faults to which this instrument with which we feel and judge can be subject. Cautiousness in judgement is nowadays to be recommended to each and every one: if we gained only one incontestable truth every ten years from each of our philosophical writers the harvest we reaped would be sufficient.

39

It is astonishing how infrequently we do what we regard as useful and would at the same time be easy to do. The desire to know a lot in a short time often hinders us from precise examination, but even the man who knows this finds it very hard to test anything with precision, even though he knows that if he does not test he will fail to attain his goal of learning more.

40

It is easy to construct a landscape out of a mass of disorderly lines, but disorderly sounds cannot be made into music.

1768–1771

1

Whenever he was required to use his reason he felt like someone who had always used his right hand but was now required to do something with his left.

2

He had an appetite for nothing yet he ate something of everything.

3

He took neither the broad nor the narrow pathway to eternity, but with frequent prayer and a good table had set out along a medium-sized one which might be called the spiritual-princely.

4

Winckelmann, Hagedorn and Lessing have communicated a wholly new spirit to our German critics. Formerly they said of a bad engraving: This engraving is a bad one – now they express their verdicts with more warmth. Of a Cœur-Dame they will speak as follows. The face has too much of one locality in it. The Juno-eyes the calendar-artist has tried to achieve possess nothing but size, they have nothing of the motionless fire that made Paris waver, nothing of the heaven in them revealed when they open and concealed when they close. The ideal character of the mouth is negated by the Frenchness of the hair, which, far from playing enviously about a full cheek, seems to be held in place by pomade and to care little whether it hides too much or too little. Her figure has about it nothing Hellenic; it might please a Moor; and one is indignant to see no sign of that slim curvature of the body which makes it seem that in turning away her face she is only offering us her warm supple bosom. The hands are as though twisted by rickets and seem to be fixed on . . . In short, we can find in the entire Cœur-Dame not the slightest trace of genius . . .*

5

In novels there occur fatal illnesses that in ordinary life are never fatal, and conversely in ordinary life fatal illnesses that are never fatal in novels.

6

In the *Spectator* it says: The whole man must move together – everything in a man must move towards the same end.

7

When we remember past pleasures we leave our physical body behind in the present and transpose ourselves back to that time entirely *in abstracto* as an Arcadian being without debts, without cares, without needy relatives: for we cannot picture to ourselves the combined effects of different impressions as easily as we can that of a single one.

8

From the sagacious regulation manifested in the instincts of animals we perhaps infer too quickly the existence of a *supremely* sagacious being: he need only be more sagacious than we are.

9

There are very few things of which we can acquire a conception through all five senses.

10

Everyone ought to study at least as much philosophy and *belles lettres* as will serve to heighten his sensual pleasures. If our country squires, courtiers, counts and others took note of this they would often be astounded at the effect a book can produce . . .

11

We can see nothing whatever of the soul unless it is visible in the expression of the countenance; one might call the faces at a large assembly of people a history of the human soul written in a kind of Chinese ideograms. As the magnet arranges iron filings, so the soul arranges around itself the facial features, and the differences in the situation of these features is determined by the differences in that which has given them this situation. The longer one observes faces the more one will perceive in so-called commonplace faces things that make them individual.

12

Every man also has his moral backside which he refrains from showing unless he has to and keeps covered as long as possible with the trousers of decorum.

13

In the house where I used to live I had got to know the sound and creak made by every step of an ancient wooden staircase, and also the rhythm produced by each of my friends who came up it to visit me; and I have to confess I always trembled when a pair of feet played an unfamiliar tune on it.

14

Character of someone I know. His body is such that even a bad draughtsman could draw it better in the dark, and if it lay in his power to alter it many parts of it would be less obtrusive. Although his health is not of the best, this man has always been more or less content with it, and he possesses to a high degree the gift of making good use of healthy days. On such days his imagination, the most loyal of his companions, never deserts him; he stands at the window with his head between his hands, and if the passer-by sees nothing but a moper with his head in his hands he himself often silently confesses he has again been indulging in an excess of pleasure. He has but few friends, in fact his heart is open only to one who is actually present, though for several who are absent; his courtesy and complaisance make many believe he is their friend, and he does indeed serve them, but it is out of ambition or philanthropy, and not from the instinct that drives him to be a servant of his real friends. He has loved only once or twice, the first time not unhappily but the second time very happily; he gained through cheerfulness and levity *alone* a good heart through which he now often forgets both, though he will always revere cheerfulness and levity as qualities of his own soul which have procured for him the pleasantest hours of his life; and if he could choose another life and another soul I do not know that he would choose different ones if he could have his own back again. Even as a boy he was very free and independent of mind as regards religion, but never thought it would do him honour to be a free-spirit, nor however that to believe everything without exception would do him honour either. He is capable of fervent prayer and has never been able to read the 90th Psalm without an indescribable feeling of exaltation. *Before the mountains were brought forth* etc. means infinitely more to him than *Sing, immortal soul* etc. He does not know whom he hates more, young officers or young clergymen, but he could not live long with either of them. For assemblies his figure and his dress have *seldom* been good enough or his sentiments sufficiently –. He hopes never to have more than three courses for lunch and two for dinner, with a little wine, or less than potatoes, apples, bread and also a little wine every day: more than the one and less than the other would both make him unwell, as they always have done when for a few days he has lived beyond their boundaries. Reading and writing are as necessary to him as eating and drinking, and he hopes he will never be without books. He thinks about death very often and never with aversion; he wishes he could think about everything with so much composure, and hopes his Creator will one day demand of him gently a life of which he was, though not a particularly economical, a by no means profligate possessor.

15

A man always writes absolutely well whenever he writes in his own manner, but the wigmaker who tries to write like Gellert . . . writes badly . . .*

16

He had recited several definitions without stumbling, and if he omitted a word he knew at once how to recover: it was his tongue rather than his reason that told him something was missing, for he had learned it all by heart.

17

He was so witty that any thing served him as an intermediate term for comparing any pair of other things with one another.

18

It is silly to assert that we are sometimes not really in the mood for anything; I believe that the moment in which we feel strong enough to suppress one of our principal drives, namely the drive to work and act, is the moment when we are perhaps best fitted to undertake the strangest and greatest things. The state we are in is a kind of languor in which the soul perceives as much that is uncommonly small as when in a state of ardent enthusiasm it does that which is uncommonly big; and as this latter state can be compared with the bold undertakings of the astronomers, so the former can be compared with the exertions of a Leeuwenhoek.*

19

Of all the animals on earth, man is closest to the ape.

20

He had outgrown his library as one outgrows a waistcoat. Libraries can in general be too narrow or too wide for the soul.

21

Human pride is a strange thing, it is not easy to suppress: when hole A has been stopped up, before you know it it is peering out of hole B, and if that is closed it is already behind hole C, etc.

22

There are two ways of extending life: firstly by moving the two points 'born' and 'died' farther away from one another ... The other method is to go more slowly and leave the two points wherever God wills they should be, and this method is for the philosophers ...

23

Division. I divide up the public in the following way: people with no wages and, poor devils, no fixed income; people who have less than 500 talers in wages or certain income; people who have more than 500 talers; people who get thousands or are of the quality. These are the four classes in the order of nature, in which class four is the greatest. I therefore solemnly declare that in my writings I have never said or thought anything against class four, indeed not even against class three, and that I shall never say or think anything that could run counter to these honorable classes. To class two I give assurance of my friendship as a fellow comrade: but class one! Behold there the field for the German satirist, a limitless field; there are poor devils everywhere and there probably will be for as long as the world endures.

24

The man of today can be conceived of as consisting of two men, the natural man and the artificial, one of whom changes in accordance with the eternal laws of nature and the other in accordance with the fickle laws of costume. In any description of man the chief thing is to distinguish the one from the other . . .

25

Sometimes I do not go out of the house for a week and live very contentedly: an equal period of house-arrest would make me ill. Where freedom is possible we move easily in our circle; where thought is under constraint even permitted thoughts come forth nervously.

26

I don't know why it is, but the word *Ionian* seems to mean much more to me than what is said in the lexicon.

27

Drinking, provided it is not indulged in before the age of 35, is not so greatly to be censured as many of my readers will imagine. This is approximately the time when a man emerges from the aberrant paths of his life out on to the plateau upon which he sees his future course lying open before him. It is depressing if, now discovering it is not the right course, he should be too weak on his feet at this stage to seek another. Should this discovery be attended by a sense of disquietude, experience has taught that wine sometimes works miracles; that five or six glasses put a man in the situation he has otherwise failed to attain . . .

28

All a little window tells us is that here too there is a place where light can enter but wind and rain are kept out.

29

If you want to take the rainwater cure you should come to Göttingen, where there is a fresh supply at all times.

30

He was then in his fifty-fourth year, when even in the case of poets reason and passion begin to discuss a peace treaty and usually conclude it not very long afterwards.

31

The only thing about him that was manly he was obliged to conceal for the sake of his comfort and well-being.

32

In the eyes of a man of the world any particular man always remains the same, whether he be a wigmaker or a minister of state, just as marble remains what it is: whether the statue represents Apollo or a Capuchin monk it cannot become bronze or sandstone.

33

To the wise man nothing is great and nothing small . . . I believe he could write treatises on keyholes that sounded as weighty as a *jus naturae* and would be just as instructive. As the few adepts in such things well know, universal morality is to be found in little everyday penny-events just as much as in great ones. There is so much goodness and ingenuity in a raindrop that an apothecary wouldn't let it go for less than half-a-crown . . .

34

He possessed a great deal of philosophy, or of common sense that looked like it.

35

He had prepared himself for what he should in any eventuality reply if the King should speak to him, even if it was only to ask his opinion of the weather; but when the King spoke to him he asked: What do they say about me in D., then? '*Rien, Monsieur,*' he replied.

36

A German who had just left Paris and was now back in his little town looked out of the window and hearing only silence exclaimed: *Mon Dieu, est ce qu'il n'y a point de bruit ici?*

37

Speech of a suicide composed shortly before the act. Friends! I stand at this moment before the veil on the point of raising it so as to see whether it will be more peaceful and quiet behind it than it is here. This is no impulse born of a mad despair: I know too well the fetters of my days from the few links in the chain I have lived through. I am too tired to go on, here I shall die clean away or at least stay overnight. Here take back the stuff that I am, nature, knead it back into the dough of being, make of me a bush, a cloud, whatever you will, even a man, only no longer make me me. Thanks be to philosophy that no pious buffooneries now disturb the train of my thoughts. Enough: I think, I fear nothing, very well, up with the curtain! –

38

Whenever I for once pause a moment and think: But if you do this you will regret it in the future – my feelings interrupt me with 'Nonsense!' and usually I have been convinced even before they have finished speaking.

39

It was a rash act, I performed it with that ardour without which my life would be worth far less than it is; I bitterly reproached myself as I finally went to bed, but my feelings were lighter by a considerable moral weight.

40

Her petticoat had stripes of broad red and blue and looked as though it had been made out of a stage-curtain. I would have paid a lot for a front seat, but there was no performance.

41

People often become scholars for the same reason they become soldiers: simply because they are unfit for any other station. Their right hand has to earn them a livelihood; one might say they lie down like bears in winter and seek sustenance from their paws.

42

An auction at which people bid with things other than money, e.g. books.

43

Drinking has, like painting, its mechanical and its poetical aspects, just as love has . . .

44

If an angel were ever to tell us anything of his philosophy I believe many propositions would sound like 2 times 2 equals 13.

45

He could not comprehend why there sometimes arose in him irresistible desires which he was none the less wholly debarred from satisfying. He often posed this question to Heaven as the subject of a prize competition and promised to reward a satisfactory answer with a complete denial of his former self and a calm and patient submission.

46

If I should ever produce an edition of his life, go straight to the index and look up the words *bottle* and *conceit*: they will contain the most important facts about him.

47

He moved as slowly as an hour-hand in a crowd of second-hands.

48

But Herr P. can certainly drink, someone said to me recently: first two bottles of wine, then 12 glasses of punch. What is his objective? If I understand him aright, it seems to me I could do all Herr P. is doing, and do it much quicker, if I fired a pistol at my head.

49

We begin reading early and we often read much too much, so that we receive and retain large amounts of material without putting it into employment and our memory becomes accustomed to keeping open house for taste and feeling; this being so, we often have need of a profound philosophy to restore to our feelings their original state of innocence, to find *our* way out of the rubble of things alien to us, to begin to feel for *ourselves* and to speak *ourselves*, and I might almost say to exist ourselves.

50

How did you enjoy yourself with these people? Answer: very much, almost as much as I do when alone.

51

Our Yoricks work in the observatories of the philosophy faculty, where we need them as much as in astronomical observatories. They do not need to master the general doctrines: they simply need to be exact observers. What would we think of an observer who published a log in which he recorded: On the 12th I saw the moon, on the 13th the sun looked very nice, the following night you could see a terrible lot of stars (et cetera)? Or who measured out the phases of a solar eclipse in Our Fathers? But most of our writers are moral observers of precisely that calibre, and the expert is as appalled when he reads it as an expert astronomer would be to read such a log.

52

What concerns me alone I only think, what concerns my friends I tell them, what can be of interest to only a limited public I write, and what the world ought to know is printed . . .

53

To learn how to teach and test yourself brings much comfort and is not as dangerous as shaving yourself; everyone should learn it at a certain age for fear of one day becoming the victim of an ill-guided razor.

54

If I did not possess an inner conviction all the honour, plaudits and good fortune of the world would give me no satisfaction, and if I am satisfied in my own conviction the condemnation of a whole world cannot deprive me of this pleasure . . .

55

I have jotted down a host of little thoughts and sketches, but they are awaiting not so much a final revision as a few more glimpses of the sun that will make them blossom.

56

It is questionable which is more difficult, to think or not to think. Man thinks by instinct, and who does not know how difficult it is to suppress an instinct? Small minds therefore truly do not deserve the contempt they are now beginning to encounter in every country.

57

It is a fault which the merely clever writer has in common with the downright bad one that he commonly fails to illuminate his actual subject but employs it only to show off. We get to know the writer but nothing else . . .

58

He had about him something the Herrnhuters commonly call exaltation, the armchair theologists call piety, and the reasonable man of the world calls simple-mindedness and want of understanding.*

59

Between dream and waking, and at the drawing near of the divinity Bacchus, the recollection of long-departed sensual delight often leaps in our souls with quite heavenly ardour.

60

To live when you do not want to is dreadful, but it would be even more terrible to be immortal when you did not want to be. As things are, however, the whole ghastly burden is suspended from me by a thread which I can cut in two with a penny-knife.

61

Of what use is it to read the authors of antiquity once a man has lost his innocence and sees his own system of thought wherever he looks? Thus the mediocre head thinks it easy to write like Horace because he considers it easy to write better and because this better is unfortunately *worse*. The older one grows (presuming one grows wiser with age) the more one loses the hope of being able to write better than the authors of antiquity; in the end one sees that the standard for all that is right and beautiful is nature and that we all bear this gauge within us but so rusted over with prejudices, with words that lack meaning, with false conceptions, that it no longer serves to gauge anything with.

62

Is it so unjust, then, that man should leave the world by the same gate through which he entered it?

63

Of all the acts of murder ever committed only those have been revealed that are known to be acts of murder.

1772–1773

The whole man must move together

1

Lady Hill, the abbess of the English convent in Lisbon, travelled in her twenty-third year to Ireland, took possession of an inheritance, and then returned to her convent. Baretti believes that such virtue in the heart of a woman deserves to be rescued from oblivion. I believe that such acts ought to be branded as hotly as imagination guided by contempt, mockery and revulsion can possibly brand them.

2

My head lies at least a foot closer to my heart than is the case with other men: that is why I am so reasonable. Resolutions can be ratified only while they are still warm.

3

Never before had a mind come to a more majestic halt.

4

Hour-glasses remind us, not only of how time flies, but at the same time of the dust into which we shall one day decay.

5

Past pain is in recollection pleasant, so is past pleasure; future pleasure is also pleasant, as is present pleasure: thus all that torments us is present and future pain – a notable preponderance of pleasure in the world, which is augmented by the fact that we continually seek to obtain pleasure and can in many cases foresee with reasonable certainty that we shall in fact obtain it, whereas pain that still lies in the future is much more rarely foreseeable

6

Something moving from one end of a grain of sand to the other with the speed of lightning or of light will seem to us to be at rest.

7

He travelled through Northeim to Einbeck and from there through Mlle P. to Hanover.

8

We often believe that our handwriting differs at different times, while to others it always looks the same.

9

If writing is now so widely seen as the measure of merit in Germany, that is thanks to a prejudice of our century. A sound philosophy will perhaps gradually dislodge this prejudice.

10

He is already in his forties and is still wearing red linings and bright colours. Thus he will never get into the lexicon of history, either as a genius or a rascal.

11

What leaning on your right elbow means after you have been leaning on your left for an hour.

12

That there are a hundred with wit for one with understanding is a true proposition with which many a witless *Dummkopf* consoles himself, when he should reflect – if that is not too much to ask of a *Dummkopf* – that there are also a hundred people possessing neither wit nor understanding for every one possessing wit.

13

'Give strength to my good resolutions' is a plea that could stand in the Lord's Prayer.

14

Diogenes, filthily attired, paced across the splendid carpets in Plato's dwelling. Thus, said he, do I trample on the pride of Plato. Yes, Plato replied, but only with another kind of pride.

15

There is a species of bird which pecks holes in the thickest hollow trees, and it credits its beak with such strength that after each peck it is said to go to the other side of the tree to see whether or not the blow has gone right through it.

16

It is, to be sure, not at all easy to teach a philosophy *answering to a practical end*: the child, the boy, the youth and the man each has his own . . . If everyone inhabited his own planet, what would philosophy then be? What it is now: the essence of a person's opinions constitutes his philosophy . . . The question 'should you philosophize yourself?' must, I think, be answered in the same way as the similar question 'should you shave yourself?' If anyone asked me I would reply: if you can do it, it's an excellent thing to do. I recall that, though we always try to teach ourselves the latter, we do not make our first attempts across the throat. Act as the wisest have acted before you, and do not commence your exercises in philosophy in those regions where an error can deliver you over to the executioner.

17

The rules of grammar are mere human statutes, which is why when he speaks out of the possessed the Devil himself speaks bad Latin.

18

That is as natural to man as thinking or throwing snowballs.

19

I once lodged in Hanover in a room whose window gave on to a narrow street which formed a communicating link between two bigger streets. It was very pleasant to see how people's faces changed when they entered the little street, where they thought they were less observed; how here one pissed, there another fixed her garter, one gave way to private laughter and another shook his head. Girls thought with a smile of the night before and adjusted their ribbons for conquests in the big street ahead.

20

The monks at Lodève, in Gascony, sanctified a mouse who had eaten a consecrated wafer.

21

A leg of mutton is better than nothing,
Nothing is better than Heaven,
Therefore a leg of mutton is better than Heaven.
In this conclusion, as in many pseudo-conclusions in which the word *nothing* occurs, it is the ambiguity of this word that is at fault. In the first line the word *nothing* excludes only those things in the world that are worse than a leg of mutton, among which 'nothing' is included; in the second line, on the other hand, the word *nothing* excludes everything in the world however great or small it may be, which again includes 'nothing'. The *nothing* of the first line is only a species of the latter from which no conclusion can be drawn regarding the genus.

22

Just as fear created gods, so an impulse for security imprinted in us creates ghosts. People who are not timorous or superstitious or cracked in the head see no spirits. The impulse for security which in a forest or at night gives me the warning: *guard yourself against attack* – this alone would suffice to produce ghosts even if there were no visionaries to hand who actually see them . . .

23

Astronomy is perhaps the science whose discoveries owe least to chance, in which human understanding appears in its whole magnitude, and through which man can best learn how small he is.

24

Every observer of human nature knows how hard it is to narrate experiences in such a way that no opinion or judgement interferes with the narration.

25

I have very often reflected on what it is that really distinguishes the great genius from the common crowd. Here are a few observations I have made. The common individual always conforms to the prevailing opinion and the prevailing fashion; he regards the state in which everything now exists as the only possible one and passively accepts it all. It does not occur to him that everything, from the shape of the furniture up to the subtlest hypothesis, is decided by the great council of mankind of which he is a member. He wears thin-soled shoes even though the sharp stones of the street hurt his feet, he allows fashion to dictate to him that the buckles of his shoes must extend as far as the toes even though that means the shoe is often hard to get on. He does not reflect that the form of the shoe depends as much upon him as it does upon the fool who first wore thin shoes on a cracked pavement. To the great genius it always occurs to ask: *could this too not be false?* He never gives his vote without first reflecting . . .

26

Herr Capitaine-Lieutenant von Hammerstein was much in favour of instruction with apparatus. The principal argument he always put forward was that it could only be a good thing to achieve one's objective as quickly as possible. That was virtually the only argument he had. But since the investigation of a subject, the effort involved in understanding it, is calculated to teach us to know it better from several sides and to attach it most readily to our system of thought, for people who have the ability a drawing is certainly to be preferred to a model. An increase in knowledge acquired too quickly and with too little participation on one's own part is not very fruitful: erudition can produce foliage without bearing fruit. There are a great many shallow heads who are astonishingly knowledgeable. What we have to discover for ourselves leaves behind in our mind a pathway that can also be used on another occasion.

27

He ate so well that a hundred people could have had their *Give us this day our daily bread* answered with what he ate.

28

The conversion of malefactors before their execution can be compared with a species of fattening: they are made spiritually fat and then have their heads cut off so that they shall not lapse again.

29

Libraries will in the end become cities, said Leibniz.

30

A punishment in a dream is still a punishment. On the utility of dreams.

31

Man does not compromise himself without expecting something in return: whence the assembling of rewards in Heaven, flagellations and the like. The philosophy of the common man is the mother of our own; our religion could grow out of his superstition as our medicine grew out of his knowledge of domestic remedies. He did something without anticipating any reward, but he received one, though he was not aware of having deserved it: what was more natural than to establish a connection between *that* desert and *this* reward? What could be more vital for the founder of a religion or more useful to society? Thus man became unselfish out of self-interest, and what fortune would have sent him anyway he accounted a payment which tied and obligated him even more.

32

You must not think, Jacobi, that your art is more important than that of the man who varnishes coffee-tables in Birmingham.*

33

Catholics do not bear in mind that the beliefs of man also change in the way their knowledge and history in general does. To increase in the one and stand still in the other is impossible to man. Even truth needs to be clad in new garments if it is to appeal to a new age.

34

We ought really to call 'a book' only that which contains something new: the rest are only a means of learning quickly what has already been done in this or that field. To discover new countries and to furnish accurate charts of what you have discovered: that is the difference. What has not yet been said on this matter?

35

Do you ask me, friend, which is better: to be plagued by a bad conscience or with a mind at peace to hang from the gallows?

36

Once the good man was dead, one wore his hat and another his sword as he had worn them, a third had himself barbered as he had, a fourth walked as he did, but the honest man that he was – nobody any longer wanted to be that.

37

The fellow wanted, before he was hanged, to see his wife again, who lived half a mile away; he asked to be allowed to go, and did so with so candid an expression that many sensible people said they believed he would return if they did let him go – for, they said, the whole demand was much too stupid to be a trick . . .

38

The pleasures of the imagination are as it were only drawings and models which are played with by poor people who cannot afford the real thing.

39

He often spoke very freely in places where everyone assumes a pious expression, but by way of compensation he preached virtue in places where no one else preached it.

40

How easily egoism can, without our noticing it, be the motivation behind many actions that seem to us wholly independent of it can be seen in the fact that people can love money as money even though they never make any use of it.

41

If there were nothing but turnips and potatoes in the world someone would perhaps say one day: what a pity the plants are upside down.

42

What Bacon says of the perniciousness of systems could be said of every word. Many words which express whole classes or every step of an entire scale are employed as though they represented a single step, that is as *individua*. This means undefining the words again.

43

You could call him the wren of the writers.*

44

The oft-repeated observation that each is best pleased by his own ought to be subjected to a lively and very philosophical scrutiny.

45

The magnet was originally of use only to conjurors.

46

I cannot blame any girl who refuses to obey the will of her parents in her choice of a husband. Shall she take something she so often beholds in the mirror, which she has so often adorned and furbished and whose decoration, cultivation and preservation has for so long been her only care – shall she take this and surrender it to someone she cannot stand?

47

A principal rule for writers, and especially those who want to describe their own sensations, is not to believe that their doing so indicates they possess a special disposition of nature in this respect. Others can perhaps do it just as well as you can. Only they do not make a business of it, because it seems to them silly to publicize such things.

48

In the matter of love, Socrates distinguished between need and passion, between the work of nature and work of the imagination. He cautioned against the latter, and for the satisfaction of the former counselled a kind of love in which the soul participated as little as possible.

49

What does it matter to you what the origin of this man's good deed may have been? Even if its source was not envy it may have been the pleasure of being envied. Not his own envy, therefore, but the envy of others.

50

Do you perhaps believe that your convictions owe their strength to arguments? Then you are certainly wrong, for otherwise everyone who hears them would have to be as convinced as you are . . . One can be deluded in favour of a proposition as well as against it. Reasons are often and for the most part only expositions of pretensions designed to give a colouring of legitimacy and rationality to something we would have done in any case . . .

51

The great also make mistakes, and some of them make so many you are almost tempted to think they weren't great at all.

52

When someone likes doing something very much he almost always has some interest in the thing that is greater than the thing itself . . .

53

The reason it is so hard to attain to something good in any of the arts and sciences is that it involves attaining to a certain stipulated point; to do something badly according to a predetermined rule would be just as hard, if indeed it would then still deserve to be called bad.

54

If people should ever start to do only what is necessary millions would die of hunger.

1773–1775

1

The learned Daille bewailed the fact that he had lost two years of his life, by which he meant the time he had spent on his travels.

2

In the words *Vox populi vox Dei* there is more truth than we usually manage to get into four words nowadays.

3

It is not hatred of vice but fear of the pillory, *or* Who can in any given case distinguish between virtue and fear of the pillory?

4

That our ancestors accorded so much importance to 'judgements of God' and attached such value to miraculous tests of innocence is certainly to be excused on account of their simplicity: their age was already sufficiently cultivated no longer to listen to prophecies but not yet sufficiently cultivated to see that to desire that God should permit the innocent to walk over red-hot iron unsinged would be contrary to his wisdom. This was reserved for our age. Nowadays certain philosophers are already beginning to make out they believe it would be contrary to God's wisdom and greatness for him to concern himself with the world at all.

5

Once we know our weaknesses they cease to do us any harm.

6

Many things about our bodies would not seem to us so filthy and obscene if we did not have the idea of nobility in our heads.

7

Anyone who had from childhood on known the masterpieces of the human mind would make an incredulous face if he read some of our moderns. It would seem to him like music played on an out-of-tune piano or on pots, pans and plates.

8

We are only too inclined to believe that if we possess a little talent work must come easily to us. You must exert yourself, man, if you want to do something great.

9

Teach me how to give substance to the salutary decisions I make, teach me to desire seriously what I desire, teach constancy when the storms of fate or the sweep of an arm shakes the building I have spent three years in raising. Teach me to speak to men's hearts without what I say doing what I did not intend to the fragile system of their convictions; and then give me the spirit of Horace as well, and thy fame shall resound through the millennia.

10

If I had not written this book then a thousand years hence between six and seven in the evening people would in many a town in Germany be talking about quite different things from what they will in fact be talking about . . .

11

That amounts to taking owls to Athens or compendia to Göttingen.

12

Whenever he composes a critical review, I have been told, he gets a tremendous erection.

13

Zezu Island. This island has remained undescribed for so long because the foolish customs of its inhabitants gave publishers everywhere the idea that an account of it was a satire on their own country . . .

14

Comedy does not effect direct improvement, and perhaps satire does not do so either: I mean one does not abandon the vices they render ludicrous. What they can do, however, is to enlarge our horizon and increase the number of fixed points from which we can orientate ourselves in all the eventualities of life more quickly.

15

I too am awakened, friend, and have attained to that degree of philosophical circumspection at which love of truth is my only guide and with the light that has been granted me go to meet all I regard as error without exclaiming *I regard that as an error*, and even less *That is error*.

16

To undertake a comparison between what we think and what we say. We may say without fear of a flogging that half the population would be flogged if they openly said what they think; and yet man is that which thinks, not that which speaks. Two people complimenting one another would at once be at loggerheads if each knew what the other thought of him.

17

What you have to do to learn to write like Shakespeare is very far removed from reading him.

18

The thought still has too much elbow-room in the expression; I have pointed with the end of a stick when I should have pointed with the point of a needle.

19

A king commands that, on pain of life imprisonment, everyone shall regard a stone as a diamond.

20

The journalists have constructed for themselves a little wooden chapel, which they also call the Temple of Fame, in which they put up and take down portraits all day long and make such a hammering you can't hear yourself speak.

21

You can take the first book you lay your hands on and with your eyes closed point to any line and say: A book could be written about this. When you open your eyes you will seldom find you are deceived.

22

As foolish as it must seem to the crab when he sees man walking forwards.

23

The inhabitants of Tahiti eat by themselves and cannot understand how it is possible to eat in company, especially with women. Banks was surprised at this and asked why they ate by themselves; they said they did so because it was the right thing to do, but why it was the right thing to do they would not and could not say.

24

The ideas and thoughts we have when awake, what are they but dreams? If while I am awake I think of friends who are dead the story proceeds without its occurring to me they are dead, as in a dream. I imagine I have won a grand lottery: at that moment I have won it, the thought that comes later that I have not won it I encounter only afterwards as an attestation of the contrary. The actual possession of something sometimes affords us no greater pleasure than the mere idea that we possess it. We can ameliorate our dreams if we abstain from meat in the evening, but what about our waking dreams? –

25

Nowadays three witty turns of phrase and a lie make a writer.

26

The first satire was certainly written for revenge. To employ it against vice for the betterment of one's fellow men rather than against the vicious is already an effete idea cooled down and made tame.

27

According to Herr Cook's observation, the inhabitants of New Guinea have something they set light to which burns up almost like gunpowder. They also put it into hollow staves, and from a distance you could believe they are shooting. But it does not produce so much as a bang. Presumably they are trying to imitate the Europeans. They have failed to realize its real purpose.

28

Like a great philosophical babbler he is concerned not so much with the truth as with the sound of his prose.

29

In trying to discover some rational meaning in incomprehensible nonsensicalities we often hit upon some good ideas: in this sense many will find Jacob Boehme's book as useful to them as the book of nature.*

30

Man is perhaps half spirit and half matter, as the polyp is half plant and half animal. The strangest of creatures lie always at the boundary.

31

Do we laugh at Jacob Boehme? But the supernatural things of which he speaks never could sound natural . . . Do we not already have in our own religion once times three equals one? . . .

32

When carrying out a piece of work always keep in mind confidence in yourself, a noble pride, and the thought that those who avoid the mistakes you make are no better than you, for they make mistakes you have avoided.

33

Describe a library situated in a madhouse, together with the librarian's remarks on the books . . .

34

It is a good thing Heaven has not given us the power to change as much of our body as we would like to or as our theory would assert is necessary . . .

35

Nowadays we already have books about books and descriptions of descriptions.

36

May Heaven forfend that I should ever write a book about books.

37

An affected earnestness that ends in a moral paralysis of the facial muscles.

38

The individual often praises what is bad, but the whole human race praises only the good.

39

It is the geniuses who, as pioneers, create the highways, and the cultivated who level and beautify them. Highway improvement would be a good thing in the sciences, so that we could get from one of them to another more easily.

40

Hume says in his essay on national characteristics that the English have of all nations least national character.

41

What was to be done in the world in Shakespeare's way Shakespeare has for the most part done.

42

Have we not been resurrected once already? Out of a condition, to be sure, in which we knew less of the present than in this present we know of the future. Our former condition is related to our present condition as our present condition is related to our future condition.

43

A man who writes a great deal and says little that is new writes himself into a daily declining reputation. When he wrote less he stood higher in people's estimation, even though there was nothing in what he wrote. The reason is that then they still expected better things of him in the future, whereas now they can view the whole progression.

44

You can be sure you are acting in accordance with the designs of nature if what you do is calculated to promote nature's great final purpose: grow and make grow. I am firmly convinced of the universality of this law.

45

Herr Professor Meister asserted that the longer the world continued the more things would be invented.*

46

I would much like to read a sermon by Herr Magister Sillig of Döbeln on whether all writers who fail to publish anything good are sinners; many of them are poor devils, that's for sure.

47

When one begins to speak of something it sounds plausible, but when we reflect on it we find it false. The initial impression a thing makes on my mind is very important. Taking an overall view of a thing the mind sees every side of it obscurely, which is often of more value than a clear idea of only one side of it.

48

God created man in his own image, says the Bible; the philosophers do the exact opposite, they create God in theirs.

49

Whether a man who writes writes well or badly can be discovered at once, but whether one who writes nothing but sits silent does so because he is sensible or because he is ignorant no mortal can discover.

50

The accomplishments of those born blind are a sure proof of how much the spirit can achieve when difficulties are placed in its way . . .

51

Really good systems of logic, says Alembert, are of use only to those who can do without them. Through a telescope the blind see nothing.

52

I imagine that when we reach the boundaries of things set for us, or even before we reach them, we can see into the infinite, just as on the surface of the earth we gaze out into immeasurable space.

53

No work, and especially no work of literature, should display the effort it has cost. A writer who wants to be read by posterity must not neglect to drop into odd corners of his chapters such hints at whole books, ideas for disputations, that his readers will believe he has thousands of them to throw away.

54

Where a body is in motion, there exists space and time, the simplest sentient creature in this world would thus be a measure of them. Our hearing, and perhaps our seeing too, consists of a counting of oscillations.

55

It is useful for a philosopher to know that men act always out of self-interest, only he must not act in accordance with this knowledge but order his actions in accordance with the usage of the world. Just as a good writer does not depart from the common usage of words, so a good citizen must not straightway depart from normal usage in the realm of actions, even though he may have much to object to in both.

56

Devised with a maximum of erudition and a minimum of common sense.

57

Our world will yet grow so subtle that it will be as ludicrous to believe in a god as it is today to believe in ghosts.

58

That man is the noblest creature may also be inferred from the fact that no other creature has yet contested this claim.

59

It requires no especially great talent to write in such a way that another will be very hard put to it to understand what you have written.

60

One of our forefathers must have read a forbidden book.

61

We should examine whether it is possible to do anything whatever having our own best interests constantly in mind.

62

What makes our poetry so contemptible nowadays is its paucity of ideas. If you want to be read, invent. Who the Devil wouldn't like to read something new?

63

One can repeat a thing in the way it has already been said, remove it further from human understanding, or bring it closer to it: the shallow mind does the first, the enthusiast the second, the true philosopher the third.

64

We have the often thoughtless respect accorded ancient laws, ancient usages and ancient religion to thank for all the evil in the world.

65

Man begins with the proposition that every quantity is equal to itself and ends by weighing the sun and the planets; here he says he is made in the image of God, and there he greedily drinks the urine of the immortal Lama; builds everlasting pyramids, Louvres, Versailles and Sanssouci, and takes delight in observing a cell in a honeycomb or a snail-shell; here he sails round the earth with the aid of a needle, and there he sits in the same spot for years on end; here he calls God the most active being, and there he calls him the Unmoving; here he reverences mice and worms as divine, there he believes in no god at all . . . What has always pleased me about man is that he, who himself constructs Louvres, everlasting pyramids and churches of St Peter, can take delight in observing a cell of a honeycomb or a snail-shell.*

66

When a book and a head collide and a hollow sound is heard, must it always have come from the book?

67

In my view this theory corresponds in psychology to a very celebrated one in physics that explains the northern lights as the phosphorescence of herrings.

68

I can hardly believe it will ever be possible to prove that we are the work of a supreme being and not rather assembled together for his own amusement by a very imperfect one.

69

The more we learn to discriminate in a language by the use of reason the harder it becomes to speak it. There is much that is instinctive in fluent speech which cannot be achieved through reason. We say that certain things have to be learned in youth: this is true of people who cultivate their reason to the detriment of all their other powers.

70

There are people who possess not so much genius as a certain talent for perceiving the desires of the century, or even of the decade, before it has done so itself.

71

If we thought more for ourselves we would have very many more bad books and very many more good ones.

72

You must never think: the proposition is too difficult for me, it is something for great scholars, I shall turn to this other one instead; this is a weakness that can easily degenerate into complete inactivity. You must not think yourself too humble for anything.

73

To discover in what way two things are related and how they behave when this common quality is attached to and detached from them.

74

The man was such an intellectual he was of almost no use.

75

I know very well the people you mean: they are all mind and theory and haven't the wit to sew on a button. Plenty of head but not hand enough to sew on a button.

76

The English follow their feelings more than other men, which is why they are so much inclined to posit novel senses: sense of truth, of moral beauty, etc.

77

Rome, London, Carthage are only more durable clouds; they all of them change and finally perish. How often we regard as essentially different from one another things that differ only in the sense of plus or minus.

78

Metaphorical language is a species of natural language which we construct out of arbitrary but concrete words. That is why it is so pleasing.

79

We have by now so many observations of man in books of travel that we could by a kind of synthesis derive from them everything any more books of travel are likely to discover.

80

In the republic of scholarship everybody wants to rule, there are no aldermen there, and that is a bad thing: every general must, so to speak, draw up the plan, stand sentry, sweep out the guardroom and fetch the water; no one wants to work for the good of another.

81

Scholars should always receive with thanks new suppositions about things, provided they possess some tincture of sense; another head may often make an important discovery prompted by nothing more than such a stimulus: the generally accepted way of explaining a thing no longer had any effect on his brain and could communicate to it no new notion.

82

He had constructed for himself a certain system which thereafter exercised such an influence on his way of thinking that those who observed him always saw his judgement walking a few steps in front of his feeling, though he himself believed it was keeping to the rear.

83

Everything grows more refined and polished: music was once noise, satire was lampoon, and where we nowadays say *Please excuse me*, in the old days we cuffed his head.

84

There are people who sometimes boast of how frank and candid they are: they ought to reflect, however, that frankness and candour must proceed from the nature of one's character, or even those who would otherwise esteem it highly must regard it as a piece of insolence.

85

You must keep two objectives constantly in mind when you are reading if you are to read wisely and judiciously: firstly to retain the matter you are reading and to unite it with your own system of thought, then above all to appropriate for your own the way in which other people have viewed this matter. That is why everyone should be warned against reading books written by bunglers, especially when they include their reasonings and arguments: you can learn of various matters from their compilations but – what is to a philosopher just as important, if not more important – you cannot learn from them how to bestow upon your mode of thinking an appropriate form.

86

I cannot deny that when I first saw that people in my fatherland were beginning to understand what radical signs are clear tears of joy sprang into my eyes.

87

Most of the expressions we use are metaphorical: they contain the philosophy of our ancestors . . .

88

If a tax had been imposed on thoughts at that time the tax would certainly have become insolvent.

89

Many people know everything they know in the way we know the solution of a riddle after we have read it or been told it, and that is the worst kind of knowledge and the kind least to be cultivated; we ought rather to cultivate that kind of knowledge which enables us to discover for ourselves in case of need that which others have to read or be told of in order to know it . . .

90

When we are seriously afraid of anything the remotest things bring it to mind. To anyone living at court the slightest movement in the face not merely of the prince himself but even of his servants can inspire a belief that he has fallen out of favour . . .

91

B: But Remus is certainly an honourable man. A: Yes he is, he has nothing else to do.

92

In England, so-called *papier mâché* decorations have become so popular I believe that in the end monuments in Westminster Abbey will be made of it. And in general it would not be a bad idea if many a scholar had the rubbishy books he has written pounded down and made into a bust of him.

93

A list of printing errors in the list of printing errors.

94

When they saw they would never be able to set a Catholic head on his shoulders they at least struck off the Protestant one.

95

In the year 1774 I read in one or other of David Hume's writings that *the English possess no character at all.* At the time I could not understand how such a man could say such a thing. Now, after having lived some 16 weeks among this people, I am thoroughly convinced that Hume is right. I do not mean to say that what he said is true, only that what last year I would have considered wholly impossible now seems to me to be the case.

96

To do the opposite of something is also a form of imitation, namely an imitation of its opposite.

97

We are obliged to regard many of our original minds as crazy at least until we have become as clever as they are.

98

A means of blowing out teeth with gunpowder.

99

The land in which *honest fellow* and *poor wretch* are terms of abuse, and *to take in* means *to deceive.*

100

She stood there beside him like an Etrurian lachrymatory, a Dresden milk-jug beside a Lauenstein beer-mug.

101

It cannot be denied that the word *nonsense*, if spoken with the appropriate face and voice, has something that yields little or nothing to the words *chaos* and *eternity* themselves. One senses a shock which, if my feelings do not deceive me, originates in a *fuga vacui* of the human understanding.

102

It is impossible to have bad taste, but many people have none at all. Most people have no ideas, says Dr Price, they talk about a thing but they don't think: this is what I have several times called *having an opinion*.

103

Body and soul: a horse harnessed beside an ox.

1775–1776

1

Ménage says that on the keystone of the gate of the royal palace in Vienna there were inscribed the vowels A.E.I.O.U., and few knew what they meant. They are the initial letters of Austriacorum Est Imperare Orbi Universo. Is that true?

2

It makes a great difference by what path we come to a knowledge of certain things. If we begin in our youth with metaphysics and religion we can easily proceed along a series of rational conclusions that will lead us to the immortality of the soul. Not every other path will lead to this, at least not quite so easily. Even though every individual word is capable of a clear definition, it is none the less impossible for us to have all these definitions before us with equal clarity in a conclusion of great complexity; when we employ them they are often combined in the manner that has been the easiest and most familiar to us from our youth onwards.

3

We have to say that the man is right, though not according to the laws we have unanimously imposed upon ourselves.

4

Every condition of the soul has its own sign and expression . . . So you will see how hard it is to seem original without being so.

5

The man exhibited such a sedate ceremoniousness in everything he said and such a bill-of-lading manner of expressing himself no living person could endure him.

6

It is very much in the order of nature that toothless animals should have horns: is it any wonder that old men and women should often have them?

7

Merchants have a waste-book (*Sudelbuch, Klitterbuch*, I think it is in German) in which they enter from day to day everything they have bought and sold, all mixed up together in disorder; from this it is transferred to the journal, in which everything is arranged more systematically; and finally it arrives in the ledger, in double entry after the Italian manner of book-keeping . . . This deserves to be imitated by the scholar. First a book in which I inscribe everything just as I see it or as my thoughts prompt me, then this can be transferred to another where the materials are more ordered and segregated, and the ledger can then contain a connected construction and the elucidation of the subject that flows from it expressed in an orderly fashion.

8

There is a great difference between *still* believing something and *again* believing it. *Still* to believe that the moon influences the plants betrays stupidity and superstition, but *again* to believe it displays philosophy and reflection.

9

He was the actual possessor of Lully's art, for he could dispute for hours on a subject without understanding a word about it.*

10

If it were true what in the end would be gained? Nothing but another truth. Is this such a mighty advantage? We have enough old truths still to digest, and even these we would be quite unable to endure if we did not sometimes flavour them with lies.

11

Nothing can contribute more to peace of soul than the lack of any opinion whatever.

12

In the happy days of barbarism one could still hope that in time one would become a good Christian. All one had to do was to go regularly to church and to give back to God a little of what one had received from him. Nowadays, however, it is hardly any longer possible to attain to the title of Christian.

13

When, in the barbaric ages, the so-called Ass Festival was celebrated in remembrance of the flight out of Egypt, instead of pronouncing the blessing the priest used to bray three times like an ass, and members of the congregation would faithfully repeat his words, some well, others badly, according to whether they were good or bad asses. This was intended, not as a joke, but as a very solemn proceeding.

14

An English farmer who was a born arithmetician once counted the words in a comedy he had been taken to see for his amusement.

15

What? to debate a subject you have to know something about it? It is my view that a debate requires that at least one of the disputants knows nothing of the subject under discussion, and that in a so-called lively debate in its highest perfection neither party knows anything about it or is even aware of the meaning of what he is saying . . . When I was in England the American question was debated in every ale-house, coffee-house, crossroads and stagecoach, and even in the council of aldermen at whose head Wilkes stood, in accordance with the rules of lively debate; and when some poor simpleton once stood up and suggested it might be a good thing to examine the subject seriously before coming to a decision, another man expressly objected that this would be a wearisome task and lead them too far astray, and that a decision should be taken without further ado – which, because it was almost dinner time, was the course agreed upon.*

16

Let him who has two pairs of trousers turn one of them into cash and purchase this book.

68

17

The man has taken the trouble to expose my mistakes; as the service he has done me is not precisely the most agreeable, I can make some claim to an indemnification. I demand no greater compensation than that he now has some of his own work printed.

18

His own figure mocks him.

19

A handful of soldiers is always better than a mouthful of arguments.

20

When we read odes our nostrils expand and so do our toes.

21

I warn everyone to beware the year 1777. London can still remember what happened in 1666.

22

I know the blue-stockings well. They are perfectly capable of making you think what is concave is in fact convex.

23

Do you thickheads perhaps believe that your exaggerated delicacy, and your dissatisfaction with what we good-naturedly do for you, is evidence of discernment in you? Oh you poor fools, there are poodles and elephants who can do as much. I myself have seen a horse who preferred Horace to Pope.

24

In the days of Henry VIII people in England had dinner at 10 in the morning and supper at four in the evening.

25

On the advance of the equinoxes and of the eating-hour. The investigation of the latter is as important to the moralist as that of the former is to the astronomer.

26

On the advance of the eating-hour. In England people in society have dinner at five. As a consequence many people no longer have supper but have instead a large breakfast at 10: what this means is that supper is by now beginning to pass over into dinner and to re-emerge as a meal (breakfast) which borrows its purpose from supper and its hour from dinner.

27

It produced the effect good books usually produce: it made the simple simpler, the clever cleverer, and all the other thousands remained unaffected.

28

Do not make a book out of material actually suited to a piece in a magazine, nor out of two words a sentence. What an idiot says in a book would be endurable if he could express it in three words.

29

A strange sound, as though a whole regiment were sneezing at the same time.

30

From love of fatherland they write stuff that gets our dear fatherland laughed at.

31

I really went to England so as to learn to write German.

32

Courage, garrulousness and the mob are on our side. What more do we want?

33

I ceased in the year 1764 to believe that one can convince one's opponents with arguments printed in books. It is not to do that, therefore, that I have taken up my pen, but merely so as to annoy them, and to bestow strength and courage on those on our own side, and to make it known to the others that they have not convinced *us*.

34

As well as body and soul he had a mask of fat, almost an inch thick, which concealed the movements of his facial muscles as effectively as other people's bodies hide their thoughts. Beneath that cover he could laugh or pull faces and no one was any the wiser.

35

Take care that accident does not place you in a situation to which you are not equal, for then you will have to appear to be what you are not: nothing is more perilous or disruptive of inward peace, indeed prejudicial to all integrity, than this is; it commonly ends in a total forfeiture of credit.

36

Know that prolixity is permissible when one is paid by the page, and I hate descriptions of a battle that take less time to read than the battle itself took. Be wary of passing the judgement: *obscure*. To find something obscure poses no difficulty: elephants and poodles find many things obscure.

37

I have held nothing back but gladly and willingly made known what with much time and sweat I have learned about mankind at almost innumerable weddings, childbeds and professorial feastings . . . and have done so without hope of the slightest profit. I have scattered the seeds of ideas on almost every page, which, if they fall on the proper soil, may bring forth chapters, or indeed whole dissertations. My language is at all times simple, select and plain, and where it is none of these three it is so as to make the translation of my treatises into English if not impossible then as difficult as I could for the German ideas-merchants in London . . .

38

For the observations of a man who, e.g., could run barefoot to Rome so as to throw himself at the feet of the Vatican Apollo I wouldn't give a penny. Such people speak only of themselves, even if they believe they are speaking of other things, and truth cannot easily get into worse hands.

39

I too have often read the descriptions I have written of my own sensations with a feeling of rapture that has covered my mortal frame with gooseflesh; with Protestant head and heart I have heard in the halls of a Catholic temple the sacred music and the thunder of verses and believed I heard in them the footsteps of the Almighty and wept tears of devotion. With inexpressible sensual pleasure I still recall the day when, walking upon the dust of kings in Westminster Abbey, I prayed to myself the words: Before the mountains were brought forth, or ever thou hadst formed the earth and the world, even from everlasting to everlasting, thou art God.

40

People cannot grasp how some can regard genius floating in the clouds, where heads glowing hot throw out half-baked ideas, as buffoonery, or indeed how one could be so cruel as to count whole chapters full of beautiful outpourings as being worth less than a single mustard-seed of matter.

41

Demonstrators where there is nothing to demonstrate. There is a kind of empty chatter which can be made to seem full through the employment of novel expressions and unexpected metaphors. Klopstock and Lavater are masters of it. As a joke it will pass. Intended seriously it is unforgivable.*

42

Truth has a thousand obstacles to overcome before it can get safely down on to paper and from paper back into a head. The liar is the least of its foes . . .

43

A sure sign of a good book is that the older we grow the more we like it. A youth of 18 who wanted and above all *could* say what he felt would say of Tacitus something like the following: Tacitus is a difficult writer who knows how to depict character: and sometimes gives excellent descriptions, but he affects obscurity and often introduces into the narration of events remarks that are not very illuminating;

you have to know a lot of Latin to understand him. At 25 perhaps, assuming he has in the interim done more than read, he will say: Tacitus is not the obscure writer I once took him for, but I have discovered that Latin is not the only thing you need to know to understand him – you have to bring a great deal with you yourself. And at 40, when he has come to know the world, he may perhaps say: Tacitus is one of the greatest writers who ever lived.

44

Margate. What happens there is what happens in every town where there are baths: you regain a little of your lost health, and lose your heart.

45

They sell everything except their shirt and then go on selling.

46

In the villages of Germany the hour of the ghosts is between 11 and 12 at night – which enables the ghosts to get to the cities in time for the city's ghost-hour, which is between eight and nine in the morning . . .

47

Our life can be compared with a winter's day: we are born between 12 and one at night, it is eight o'clock before day dawns and dark again before four in the afternoon, and at 12 we die.

48

If mankind suddenly became virtuous, many thousands would die of hunger.

49

A book is a mirror: if an ape looks into it an apostle is hardly likely to look out. We have no words for speaking of wisdom to the stupid. He who understands the wise is wise already.

50

Man is not so hard to know as many a stay-at-home believes when in his dressing-gown he rejoices to discover that one of Rochefoucauld's remarks is true. I believe, indeed, that most people know men better than they themselves are aware of, and that they make great use of their knowledge in everyday life ...

51

It is no great art to say something briefly when, like Tacitus, one has something to say; when one has nothing to say, however, and none the less writes a whole book and makes truth, with its *ex nihilo nihil fit*, into a liar – that I call an achievement.

52

As I take up my pen I feel myself so full, so equal to my subject, and see my book so clearly before me in embryo, I would almost like to try to say it all in a single word.

53

The man who believed a compendium was a book and that to record facts was to write history.

54

Nature has joined men at the heart, and the professors would like them to be joined at the head.

55

The great rule: If the little bit you have is nothing special in itself, at least find a way of saying it that is a little bit special.

56

You must not look for order in this little book. Order is a daughter of reflection, and my enemies have devoted so little reflection to me I cannot see why I should devote any to them.

57

There they sit, with hands folded and eyes closed, and wait for Heaven to bestow on them the spirit of Shakespeare ... [But] the basis of everything is observation and knowledge of the world, and you have to have observed a great deal yourself if you are to be able to employ the observations of others as though they were your own ...

58

He cannot even distinguish between passive and active reading.

59

There are people who believe everything is sane and sensible that is done with a solemn face.

60

Faugh! to dwell on such trifles is to bring up a batter of artillery against a flock of wagtails: sensible people will find it hard to say whether you delivered the blow or received it.

61

Is that a sin? as little as throwing stones at a window or stealing apples.

62

When they have discovered truth in nature they fling it into a book, where it is in even worse hands.

63

Oh, that must be one of the three wise men of Switzerland.

64

Proposal: in a cold winter why not burn books?

65

Do we write books so that they shall merely be read? Don't we also write them for employment in the household? For one that is read from start to finish, thousands are leafed through, other thousands lie motionless, others are jammed against mouseholes, thrown at rats, others are stood on, sat on, drummed on, have gingerbread baked on them or are used to light pipes with.

66

A good expression is worth as much as a good idea, because it is almost impossible to express oneself well without throwing a favourable light on that which is expressed.

67

Now that we know nature thoroughly, a child can see that in making experiments we are simply paying nature compliments. It is no more than a ceremonial ritual. We know the answers in advance. We consult nature in the same way as great rulers consult their parliaments.

68

I am truly not joking, my dear countrymen, when I confess that the Germans have no *esprit*, for the little bit of playing at atheism we indulge in cannot be called *esprit*. A French atheist with *esprit* is expected to be converted only when he is seriously ill or on his deathbed, whereas ours are usually converted every time there is a thunderstorm. Nor are the scribblings of our youth evidence that our youth possess *esprit*: *esprit* is nonsense, to be sure, but not every kind of nonsense is *esprit*.

69

The obscure feeling of perfectability that he has causes man to think he is still far from his goal when he has in fact attained it but the light of reason is not bright enough for him. What he finds easy he thinks bad, and thus he strains from the bad to the good and from the good to a kind of bad that he considers better than good. Good taste is either that which agrees with my taste or that which subjects itself to the rule of reason. From this we can see how useful it is to employ reason in seeking out the laws of taste.

70

To desire to draw the nightwatchman after the sound of his voice. The result is often so wrong we cannot help laughing when we see our mistake. Is physiognomy any different? The people in whose company we travel by night in a stagecoach.

71

'How's it going?' a blind man asked a cripple. 'As you see,' the cripple replied.

72

A man can condemn a good book as bad out of envy, want of judgement, or folly, but Man cannot ... A man can commend something bad and condemn something good, but Man cannot.

73

It is pity and fear that Aristotle saw as the objective of tragedy, not pity and terror.

74

One must not break up too much, not abstract too much: the great *raffineurs* have, I believe, made the fewest discoveries. The utility of the human machine is precisely that it delivers totals.

75

The art of bringing out a work at the right time is possessed chiefly by our own fatherland: they know how to enter between too soon and too late with such precision you couldn't squeeze a day in. For they cannot come sooner, since they are not yet ready, and not later because then everyone would usually already know what was in them.

76

With a pen in my hand I have successfully stormed bulwarks from which others armed with sword and excommunication have been repulsed.

77

Our philosophers hear too little of the voice of feeling; or rather, they seldom possess sufficient sensibility not to respond to every occurrence more with what they know than with what they feel; and that is worthless, it takes us not one step nearer to true philosophy. Is what man can know necessarily what he ought to know?

78

Who would wish to say how far the perfectability of man can go? From the child who reels and staggers on his nurse's hand to Terzi in London, who would wish to assert that men will never learn to fly? ...*

79

Even if they were of use for nothing else, the poets of antiquity at least enable us here and there to get to know the opinions of the common people . . . For our folksongs are often full of a mythology known to no one but the fool who made the folksong.

80

Götz von Berlichingen will no more be played at Drury Lane than the cardinals will sing a *Landes-Vater* in St Peter's.*

81

The man goes too far, but do I not do so too? He likes to hear himself in his enthusiasm. Do I not like to hear myself being witty? or expressing my cold-blooded contempt for all that is done out of enthusiasm?

82

The Jews ought to hail Lavater as the Messiah.

83

The English obey their feelings more than other men do, which is why they are so much inclined to posit novel senses: sense of truth, of moral beauty, etc.

84

A chief rule in philosophy is to produce no *deus ex machina*, to assume no sense or instinct where you can still make do with association and mechanism.

85

People who have read a great deal seldom make great discoveries. I do not say this to excuse laziness, for invention presupposes an extensive contemplation of things on one's own account; one must see for oneself more than let oneself be told.

86

A person's actions, the constitution of his household, are commonly continuations of his own inner constitution, of his brain, etc. In the way the magnet bestows form and order on iron filings.

87
In Germany sewing-needles hear and in England they see.*

88
If people would recount their dreams honestly, character could be divined more easily from them than from the face.

89
The utility of systems lies not merely in their making us think about something in an ordered way according to a particular scheme but in their making us think about it at all; the latter utility is incontestably greater than the former.

90
Herr Professor Koppe was with me; he told me that Herr Goethe preferred to associate with an original fool rather than with a sensible man. Celle might thus be the best place for him.

91
We do not think good metaphors are anything very important, but I think a good metaphor is something even the police should keep an eye on . . .

92
What I do not like about our definitions of genius is that there is in them nothing of the day of judgement, nothing of resounding through eternity and nothing of the footsteps of the Almighty.

93
What effect must it have on a nation if it learns no foreign languages? Probably much the same as that which a total withdrawal from all society has on an individual.

94

There is no surer way of making a name for oneself than by writing about things which appear to be important but which a sensible man would rarely take the time to investigate.

95

A on his lips and *not-A* in his heart.

1776–1779

1

If it is permissible to write plays that are not intended to be seen, I should like to see who can prevent me from writing a book no one can read.

2

If you want to know what other people think about something that concerns you, you have only to reflect on what you would think of them under the same circumstances. You should regard no one as morally superior to you on this point, and no one as more simple. More often than we think, people notice things we believe we have artfully concealed from them. Of this remark more than half is true, and that is saying a lot of a maxim composed in one's thirtieth year.

3

Expressions of magnanimity are nowadays more a product of learning, or rather: people are magnanimous in order to exhibit their learning rather than from goodness of heart. People who are magnanimous by nature seldom notice there is anything special about being magnanimous.

4

I am convinced that if God should ever create a man as our masters of arts and our professors of philosophy imagine man to be he would be taken to the madhouse on the first day of his life . . .

5

What a work could be written on Shakespeare, Hogarth and Garrick! There is something similar in the genius of all three: intuitive knowledge of men of every class made comprehensible through words, engraving tool and gesture respectively.

6

As soon as one begins to see all in everything what one says usually becomes obscure. One begins to speak with the tongues of angels . . .

7

Every stick of sealing-wax reminded him of the faithlessness of man and of Adam's fall.

8

The most heated defenders of a science, who cannot endure the slightest sneer at it, are commonly those who have not made very much progress in it and are secretly aware of this defect.

9

To make clever people believe we are what we are not is in most instances harder than really to become what we want to seem to be.

10

The welfare of many countries is decided by a majority of votes, even though everyone admits there are more wicked men than good ones.

11

Bon sens, Menschen-Verstand, common sense is too often regarded as a perfect organ of knowledge; in fact, however, it is nothing more than an ever wakeful intuitive perception of the truth of useful general propositions.

12

Every trade demands a reasonable period of apprenticeship. I doubt, however, whether our geniuses could throw themselves into the trade of shoemaker as speedily as they throw themselves into the profession of criticism . . . They ought to consider that there are people who can judge a work of the imagination as quickly and at the same time accurately as others can a shoe . . .

13

Most of our writers possess, I do not say insufficient genius, but insufficient sense to write a *Robinson Crusoe*.

14

They sneezed, wheezed, coughed and made two other kinds of sound for which we have no words in German.

15

Every poor devil ought to have at least two honest names, so that he can put the one at risk to provide bread for the other. That is why writers sometimes write anonymously . . .

16

The frogs were much happier under King Log than they were under King Stork.

17

A book is a mirror: if an ape looks into it an apostle is unlikely to look out.

18

Rogues would be more dangerous, or a new species of dangerous rogue would appear, if people began to study law in order to steal . . .

19

A few weeks ago a man came to see me in Göttingen who could make a new pair of silk stockings out of two old pairs, and offered me his services. We understand the art of making a new book out of a pair of old ones.

20

Mixing with rational people is so greatly to be recommended to everyone because in this way even a blockhead can learn to act sensibly by mimicry: for the greatest blockheads are able to mimic, even apes, poodles and elephants can do it.

21

Why are unpleasant thoughts so much more painful first thing in the morning when you have just woken up than they are some time afterwards when you know everyone is awake, or when you have got up, or in the middle of the day, or at night when you go to bed? I have had this happen to me often: I have gone to bed at night quite untroubled about certain things and then started to worry fearfully about them at about four in the morning, so that I often lay tossing and turning for several hours, only to grow indifferent or optimistic again at nine or even earlier.

22

What are our learned journals and most of our magazines? They differ from a mere catalogue of books, to be sure, but what makes them differ from a catalogue of books is precisely that which ensures that almost no one reads them any more.

23

To write with sensibility requires more than tears and moonlight.

24

Something witty can be said against anything and for anything. A witty man could, of course, say something against this assertion that would perhaps make me regret it.

25

There is another way of lengthening one's life that lies wholly within our power. Rise early, purposeful employment of our time, selection of the most suitable means for achieving an end we have in view and its vigorous employment once it is selected. It is possible to grow very old in this way provided we have ceased to measure our life by the calendar . . . Once you have decided to undertake a piece of work it is not a good thing to keep the whole of it before your mind; I at least have found doing so very disheartening. What you should do is work at that which lies immediately to hand, and when that is finished go on to the next . . . To start on a thing straightaway without putting it off for a minute, much less an hour or a day, is likewise a way of making time expand.

26

The forests are getting smaller and smaller, the amount of wood is decreasing, what shall we do? Oh, when the time comes that the forests cease to exist we shall certainly be able to burn books until new ones have grown.

27

To imagine the world so greatly magnified that particles of light look like 24-lb cannonballs.

28

There are names that ought to be stamped on every gallows in the world.

29

Perhaps a dog just before it goes to sleep or a drunken elephant has ideas that would not be unworthy of a Master of Philosophy. But such ideas are useless to them, and their all too sensitive sensual apparatus soon expunges them.

30

The judgements of the world are always too favourable or too unfair.

31

Experience, not reading and listening, is the thing. It is not a matter of indifference whether an idea enters the soul through the eye or through the ear.

32

The first rule with novels as well as plays is to regard the various characters as though they were pieces in a game of chess and not seek to win one's game by changing the laws that govern these pieces – not move a knight like a pawn, etc. Secondly, to define these characters exactly and not render them inactive in order to reach one's final goal but rather to win by allowing them to be what they are. To do otherwise really means wanting to work miracles, which are always unnatural.

33

If countries were named after the words you first hear when you go there, England would have to be called *Damn It*.

34

Long before we could explain the common phenomena of the physical world we ventured to explain them through the agency of spirits. Now we know better how they are linked together we explain one phenomenon by means of another; but we none the less still have two spirits left to us, a god and a soul. The soul is thus even now, as it were, the ghost that haunts our body's fragile frame. But is this adequate even for our limited reason: must that which, in our opinion, cannot be brought about by the things we know be brought about by things other than those we know? This is not only a false but a tasteless process of reasoning. I am altogether convinced that we know precisely nothing of that which is comprehensible to us, and how much more may there not be that the fibres of our brain cannot picture? What most becomes us in philosophy, and especially in psychology, is modesty and circumspection. What is matter as the psychologist thinks of it? Perhaps nothing of the sort exists in nature; he kills matter and afterwards says it is dead.

35

Honest unaffected distrust of human abilities under all circumstances is the surest sign of strength of mind.

36

There are people who are born with a bad conscience . . .

37

What they call 'heart' lies much lower than the fourth waistcoat-button.

38

Leibniz defended the Christian religion: to conclude straightway from that that he was a good Christian, as the theologians do, betrays very little knowledge of the world. The vanity of doing better than the professionals is in the case of a man such as Leibniz, who had few principles, a much more likely motivation for doing such a thing than religion would be. If we search more deeply into our own bosom we shall discover how little of the sort can be asserted of others either. I dare say, indeed, that I could demonstrate that we often believe we believe something and yet we do not believe it. Nothing is more unfathomable than the system of motivations behind our actions.

39

If you are going to build something in the air it is always better to build castles than houses of cards.

40

I believe that the source of most human misery lies in softness and indolence. The nation with the greatest vibrancy has always been also the freest and happiest. Indolence takes no revenge but accepts every kind of affront and every kind of oppression.

41

The metaphor is much more subtle than its inventor, and so are many things. Everything has its depths. He who has eyes sees all in everything.

42

Just as a deaf-mute can learn languages and how to read, so we too can do things whose compass we do not know and accomplish designs we are unaware of. He is a witness for a sense he himself does not have.

43

Men do not go on all fours, to be sure, but they go with all fours; no one can run fast without making a similar movement with his arms. Many people swing their arms when they walk, not imitatively but by nature: the same force that moves their legs seems at the same time to move their arms; and when people jump they make a leaping movement with their arms.

44

The Greeks possessed a knowledge of human nature we seem hardly able to attain to without passing through the strengthening hibernation of a new barbarism.

45

Why are young widows in mourning so beautiful? (Look into it.)

46

The oracles have not so much ceased to speak, rather men have ceased to listen to them.

47

We say that someone occupies an official position, whereas it is the official position that occupies him.

48

Man seeks freedom where it would make him unhappy, in political life, and rejects it where it makes him happy and adheres blindly to the opinions of others. The despotism of religion and doctrine is the most fearful of all despotisms. The Englishman who inveighs against the government is a slave of the opposition, a slave of fashion, of foolish customs, of etiquette.

49

Man can acquire accomplishments or he can become an animal, whichever he wants. God makes the animals, man makes himself.

50

Many a man torments himself his whole life long, studies himself frigid and impotent, at unravelling a writer's meaning. I admit that it needs a lifetime to unravel the writer's system and to cleanse it of the dirt and grease of those who have sought to patch and improve it; all this is true, yet it would require only fifteen minutes of wide-awake common sense to see that the whole thing isn't worth three-halfpence.

51

Thinking for oneself is often recommended only for the purpose of studying how to distinguish between truth and the errors other people make. That is certainly useful, but is it all? . . . Someone once said with great truth that though printing had certainly propagated learning it had also reduced its content. Much reading is harmful to thinking. The greatest thinkers I have known have been precisely those who of all the scholars I have known had read least. Is enjoyment of the senses nothing whatever, then?

52

Most scholars are more superstitious than they say, more indeed than they themselves believe. It is not so easy to break bad habits completely, though we can conceal them from the world and prevent them from having harmful consequences.

53

Doubt must be no more than vigilance, otherwise it can become dangerous.

54

I am convinced we do not only love ourselves in others but hate ourselves in others too.

55

The natural scientists of the previous age knew less than we do and believed they were very close to the goal: we have taken very great steps in its direction and now discover we are still very far away from it. With the most rational philosophers an increase in their knowledge is always attended by an increased conviction of their ignorance.

56

'What you are looking for is usually in the last pocket you look in' is an alleged empirical proposition which has, I believe, been assumed true in every land and every family: and yet no one seriously believes it.

57

Wine is accredited only with the misdeeds it induces: what is forgotten is the hundreds of good deeds of which it is also the cause. Wine excites to action: to good actions in the good, to bad in the bad.

58

Whenever he spoke every mousetrap in the neighbourhood snapped shut.

59

Man becomes a sophist and over-acute whenever he lacks true and thorough knowledge; consequently everyone must do so when it comes to the immortality of the soul and life after death. Here we are all superficial. Materialism is the asymptote of psychology.

60

With our fashionable poets it is so easy to see how the word has produced the thought; with Milton and Shakespeare the thought always begets the word.

61

It is as though our languages were in a state of confusion: when we want an idea they bring us a word, when we require a word they bring us a dash, and when we expected a dash there stands an obscenity.

62

Man has an irresistible instinct to believe he is not seen when he himself sees nothing. Like children who shut their eyes so as not to be seen.

63

A bound book of blank paper has a charm all of its own. Paper that has not yet lost its virginity and is still decked in the colour of innocence is always preferable to paper that has been used.

64

The publisher has had him hanged in effigy in front of his work.

65

In Göttingen there is no formal theatre, to be sure, but that only makes it all the easier to put together a comedy for oneself: a scene here, a scene there.

66

If physiognomy becomes what Lavater expects it to become, children will be hanged before they have perpetrated the deeds that deserve the gallows; a new kind of confirmation will thus be performed every year. A physiognomical *auto-da-fé*.

67

I cannot say I have been his enemy, but neither have I been his friend: I have never so much as dreamed of him.

68

Liskow says that the dreadful crowd of bad writers we have is every bit as able to plunge us into a state of barbarism as is a horde of Ostrogoths and Visigoths. (Excellently said.)

69

A clever child brought up with a foolish one can itself become foolish. Man is so perfectable and corruptible he can become a fool through good sense.

70

Ideas too are a life and a world.

71

There are people of an innocuous disposition who are at the same time vain, who speak constantly of their honesty and pursue it almost like a profession, and who know how to whine about their merits with such boastful modesty one loses all patience with these perpetually importunate creditors.

72

If what I once read is true, that no one dies without first having said something of sense, then M. has produced one of the immortals.

73

I have remarked very clearly that I am often of one opinion when I am lying down and of another when I am standing up . . .

74

To excuse one's own failings as being only human nature is, provided one has meant well, every writer's first duty to himself.

75

With the band that should have tied their hearts together they have strangled their tranquillity.

76

He stood there looking as sad as a dead bird's bird-bath.

77

In former days when the soul was still immortal.

78

All impartiality is artificial. Man is always partial and is quite right to be. Even impartiality is partial. He was of the party of the impartial.

79

That which we are able to judge with our feelings is very little and simple; everything else is all prejudice and complaisance.

80

There are fanatics without ability, and then they are really dangerous people.

81

There is no more important rule of conduct in the world than this: attach yourself as much as you can to people who are abler than you and yet not so very different that you cannot understand them . . .

82

If we make a couple of discoveries here and there we need not believe things will go on like this for ever. An acrobat can leap higher than a farm-hand, and one acrobat higher than another, yet the height no man can overleap is still very low. Just as we hit water when we dig in the earth, so we discover the incomprehensible sooner or later.

83

It is a *fallacia conclusionis a dicto secundum quid ad dictum simpliciter*: precisely the error into which the Devil fell when he believed he could persuade Christ to throw himself down from the pinnacle of the temple.

84

There exists a species of transcendental ventriloquism by means of which men can be made to believe that something said on earth comes from Heaven.

85

'What a pity it isn't a sin to drink water,' cried an Italian, 'how good it would taste.'

86

Everything has its workaday side and its Sunday side.

87

Amplify the following proposition: Just as the performance of the vilest and most wicked deeds requires spirit and talent, so even the greatest demand a certain insensitivity which under other circumstances we would call stupidity.

88

Much can be inferred about a man from his mistress: in her one beholds his weaknesses and his dreams . . .

89

I ask no quarter and will give no quarter to anyone who attacks me unjustly, no matter who he is. Freedom to think and write the truth is a prerogative of the town where George rules and upon which Münchhausen's blessing reposes. We may here say aloud: A fool is a fool – whether he lies in chains or is worshipped and adored.

90

Of that which man ought to be even the best of us know little that can be relied on; of that which he is we can learn something from everybody.

91

To give another example of a sign of the possession of understanding that has seldom deceived me, I have found that people who are much older than they appear to be seldom possess much understanding, and conversely young people who look old also come close to the understanding possessed by age. You will understand that by looking young I do not mean possessing health and a healthy colour, nor by the appearance of age the possession of a face lined and wan.

92

Our thoughts would take an altogether different course if things other than reflection were not operating within us: every man would have his own morality as well as his own face . . .

93

Opportunity does not make only thieves, it also makes popular people, philanthropists, heroes; of the inspiration that strikes the witty man more than half belongs to the blockhead he has encountered.

94

It always rains when it is market day or when we hang washing out to dry, what we are looking for is always in the last pocket we put our hand into.

95

I again commend dreams; we live and experience in dreams as well as we do when awake . . . The dream is a life which, combined with the rest of our life, constitutes what we call human life. Dreams merge gradually into our waking state: one cannot say where a man's waking state begins.

96

A pleasing voice is very often united with other good qualities of body and soul. And yet so many female singers are whores, and most people can't sing.

97

It is just as easy to dream without sleeping as it is to sleep without dreaming.

98

In the matter of seeing without light, it is noteworthy that what we see if we close our eyes in the dark can become the beginnings of dreams, only what follows is quite different according to whether we then sleep or stay in possession of our waking reason. I should like to know whether animals' dreams are stupider than the animals are when awake: if so, they possess a degree of reason.

99

I believe it is much better to draw forth out of ourselves than out of Plato: we can misunderstand Plato, but we are at all times *close enough* to ourselves to assuage all difficulties and illumine all that is obscure.

100

Sickness is mankind's greatest defect.

101

If reason, the daughter of Heaven, were allowed to be the judge of beauty, only sickness would be ugly.

102

Truth will find a publisher at any time, complaisance usually only for a year. That is why when you write you should always do so with courage and candour.

103

That Garve has ceased to write is as great a loss to our literature as that Lavater has started to.

104

That the earth goes round the sun and that when I sharpen a pen the point of it flies off into my eye is all one law.

105

I believe precisely the opposite, namely that most of the good in the world is done by people in no way noted for their culture and refinement. And that most of the mischief in the world has been caused by beauty. Even though it may have promoted the happiness, or rather the sensual pleasure, of individuals.

106

For a long time now I have been writing a history of my mind and of my wretched body, and that with an honesty which will perhaps awaken in many a kind of fellow shame; it is to be told with a greater degree of honesty than any of my readers will perhaps believe. This is a hitherto little frequented path to immortality . . .

107

This incomprehensible being we are, and which would appear even more incomprehensible to us if we could come even closer to it, we must not expect to find inscribed on a countenance.

108

The detection of small errors has always been the property of minds elevated little or not at all above the mediocre; notably elevated minds remain silent or say something only in criticism of the whole, while the great spirits refrain from censuring and only create.

109

People do not like to take ticket No. 1 in a lottery. Take it, reason cries aloud, it can win the 12,000 talers just as well as any other; don't take it for the world, a *je ne sais quoi* whispers, it has never been known for such small numbers to appear beside big winnings – and as a result we don't take it.

110

In as complicated a machine as this world is, it seems to me that, all our little contributory efforts notwithstanding, we are in all essentials always participating in a lottery.

111

To think this causes a confusion in my head, almost as though I sought to think that Poland lies to the west of us.

112

That men so often make false judgements is certainly not to be attributed solely to a lack of insight and ideas, but principally to the fact that they do not place every element of the proposition under the microscope and reflect on it.

113

Thousands can see that a proposition is nonsense without possessing the capacity formally to refute it.

114

Jena and Gomorrha.*

115

Sometimes we make in the morning a statment that afterwards dogs us for the rest of the day: thus on 28 February 1778 I said once almost every quarter of an hour: *Law is a bottomless pit*.

116

I am much more compassionate in my dreams than I am when awake.

117

A pure heart and a clean shirt. (A pure heart is an excellent thing, and so is a clean shirt.)

118

The infirm often possess accomplishments which a man of sound constitution is either incapable of or lacks the resolution to acquire.

119

Two people, one of whom wanted to convert the other and had failed to do so, unite together to convert me, and will have a hard job to do so.

120

The most successful tempters and thus the most dangerous are the deluded deluders.

121

An amen face.

122

Whenever *cultivated* men of the world say God knows! it is always a sure sign that in addition to Almighty God they know an almighty man who also knows.

123

What is the good of drawing conclusions from experience? I don't deny we sometimes draw the right conclusions, but don't we just as often draw the wrong ones? And isn't that what I was trying to say? A game of chance.

124

An ass was obliged to carry the image of Isis, and when the people fell down and worshipped the image he thought they were honouring him.

125

Janet Macleod is the name of a girl who for many years on end ate nothing . . . People who except for a couple of magazine-crumbs have taken no mental food for ten years exist even among professors – it is, in fact, not at all uncommon.

126

Something may be made even of dogs if they are brought up properly; only you must have them associate, not with mature people, but with children: thus they will become human. This is a confirmation of my proposition that children should always be attached to people who are *only a little* wiser than they themselves are.

127

Not at all is from a human point of view always no more than *very little*. *Not at all* belongs in general only to the angels, *very little* is what belongs rather to men.

128

Oh, here it was only last September they learned Herculaneum had been rediscovered.

129

What can be the reason I sometimes fret about a thing at nine o'clock, cease to do so at ten, and perhaps do so again at eleven? I am not aware of any ebb and flow of grounds of solace during this time, yet such there must be.

130

That which creates the polymath is often not a knowledge of many things but a happy relationship between his abilities and his taste by virtue of which the latter always approves of what the former produces.

131

With many a work of a celebrated man I would rather read what he has crossed out than what he has let stand.

132

The world offers us correction more often than consolation.

133

God, who winds up our sundials.

134

Certain rash people have asserted that, just as there are no mice where there are no cats, so no one is possessed where there are no exorcists.

135

How perfectable man is, and how necessary instruction is, can be seen simply from the fact that man now appropriates in sixty years a culture upon which the whole race has spent five thousand years. A youth of eighteen is able to contain within him the wisdom of entire ages. If I learn the proposition: *the force that attracts in polished amber is the same that thunders in the clouds* – which I can do very quickly – I have learned something the discovery of which cost mankind several thousand years.

136

First there is a time when we believe everything without reasons; then for a short time we believe but with discrimination; then we believe nothing at all; and then we again believe everything and go on to specify our reasons for believing everything.

137

We cannot prove that the planets are inhabited by rational creatures: none the less I believe it. Thus anyone can believe that the soul dies with the body, even though he cannot strictly prove it.

138

You have discovered these traits together ten times, but have you also counted the times you have not found them together?

139

A droll thought: a scholar weeping because he cannot understand his own writings.

140

We must not seek to abstract from the busts of the great Greeks and Romans rules for the visible form of genius as long as we cannot contrast them with Greek blockheads.

141

If you want to make a young person read a certain book you must not so much commend it to him directly as praise it in his presence. He will then go and find it for himself.

142

The drive to propagate our race has also propagated a lot of other things.

143

When something bites us in the dark we can usually locate the spot with the point of a needle: how exact a plan of its body the soul must have.

144

Much reading has brought upon us a learned barbarism.

145

It is incontestible that male beauty has not yet been sufficiently depicted by the hands that alone could have depicted it, namely female hands. I am always pleased to hear of a new poetess: provided she has not modelled her work on poems written by men, what discoveries could await us!

146

I have sometimes rejoiced in myself when people who thought themselves philosophers and keen observers of human nature have passed judgement on me. How dreadfully wrong they are: the one considered me far better and the other far worse than I really was, and always, as he thought, on very fine and subtle grounds.

147

There are people who always write the word Devil with a D and a succession of dots. They likewise render this mark of respect to certain parts of their own body. The cause of this is hard to discover. Even Fielding writes Kiss my a--- instead of Kiss my arse. Presumably in this case it amounts to the same thing as putting on a pair of trousers.

148

In addition to his spiritual flock from which he took something whenever he could, he had another two hundred head out at pasture which he regularly fleeced.

149

Affectation is a very good word when someone does not wish to confess to what he would none the less like to believe of himself.

150

There are few people who do not believe many things which they would, if they subjected them to closer examination, find they did not understand. They believe merely on the word of many other people, or think they lack the ancillary knowledge which if they acquired it would abolish all doubt. Thus it is possible for there to be a universal belief in a proposition whose truth no man has yet tested.

151

As soon as we know anyone is blind we believe we could see that from behind him.

152

It is necessary for a writer to go out into the world, not so much to observe many situations as to get into many situations himself.

153

When one condemned to death is given another hour it is worth a lifetime.

154

That people who read so astonishingly should often be such bad thinkers may likewise have its origin in the constitution of our brain. It is certainly not a matter of indifference whether I learn something without effort or finally arrive at it myself through my system of thought. In the latter case everything has roots, in the former it is merely superficial.

155

When an acquaintance goes by I often step back from my window, not so much to spare him the effort of acknowledging me as to spare myself the embarrassment of seeing that he has not done so.

156

There are certainly few duties in the world as important as promoting the continuation of the human race and preserving ourselves, for there are none to which we are drawn so strongly as we are to these two.

157

Let us take Sir Isaac Newton. All discoveries are due to chance, whether towards the end or the beginning of the process, for otherwise reasonable people could sit down and make discoveries as one sits down and writes a letter. The imagination spots a similarity and reason tests it and finds it true: *that is discovery*. That is how Sir Isaac Newton was. I have not the slightest reason to doubt that there existed before him and after him, in England and without, and that there exist now minds superior to his in ability, just as I have no reason to doubt that the peasant who gazes in admiration at the preacher would preach better than he if he had studied and acquired the knack. Opportunity and occasion are the discoverer and ambition the improver, confidence in one's own strength is strength, in marriage and in the world of learning.

158

In philosophy this is often the case: If all are not something then none is that something, inasmuch as anything is true only through being a plus or minus of other things. [*Wenns nicht alle sind, so ists gar keiner indem es von den andern nur durch plus und minus wahr ist.*]

159

Before you damn to Hell any great criminal whose story you have read just give thanks to benevolent Heaven that it did not place *you*, with your fair and honest face, at the commencement of such a succession of circumstances.

160

You believe I run after the strange because I do not know the beautiful; no, it is because you do not know the beautiful that I seek the strange.

161

I can easily imagine how easily a person can be seduced by newspaper praise into in the end believing he really is what these people say he is. Complaisance gives birth to complaisance . . .

162

I experience a very unpleasant sensation if anyone takes pity on me, as the word is commonly used. That is why when people are really angry with someone they employ the expression: such a person is to be pitied. This kind of pity is a species of charity, and charity presupposes need on the one side and superfluity on the other . . .

163

(Lion) . . . could from his 16th year no longer convince himself that Christ was the son of God, and this became so commonplace a thing to him and grew to be so much a part of him as he grew that such a conviction was no longer so much as thinkable. His only regret was that Christ himself had not written a book . . .*

164

Waste-book method highly recommended. A note made of every phrase, every expression. Wealth can also be acquired through saving up truths in pennyworths.

165

(Lion) fell in love in his 10th year with a boy named Schmidt (best pupil in the school), the son of a tailor, liked to hear him talked about and got all the boys to converse with him, never spoke to him himself but it gave him great pleasure to hear that the boy had spoken of him. Climbed up on a wall after school to see him go out of school. Now he still remembers his physiognomy very clearly, and he was far from handsome, a turned-up nose and red cheeks. But he was first in the school. I should be sorry if by this free confession I should increase the world's mistrust, but I was a human being and if happiness is ever to be attained in this world it must not be sought through concealment, not at all, nothing firm can come about in that way. Lasting happiness is to be found only in uprightness and sincerity . . .

166

The most brightly coloured birds sing the worst; the same goes for people . . .

1779–1783

1

To make known the weaknesses of the great is a kind of duty: in doing so one comforts thousands without doing the great any harm. D'Alembert's letter on Rousseau in the *Mercure de France*, September 1779, deserves to be better known.

2

People nowadays have such hopes of America and the political conditions obtaining there that one might say the desires, at least the secret desires, of all enlightened Europeans are *deflected to the west*, like our magnetic needles.

3

Herr Camper related that when a missionary painted the flames of Hell to a congregation of Greenlanders in a truly vivid fashion, and described at length the heat they gave out, all the Greenlanders began to feel a strong desire to go to Hell.

4

It is almost impossible to bear the torch of truth through a crowd without singeing somebody's beard.

5

The soup tasted so foul that to believe it had been deliberately poisoned you would have needed only to be a king or a great general.

6

A woman's eyes are to me so essential a part of her, I often gaze at them and have so many thoughts, that if I were merely a head girls could for my part be nothing but eyes.

7

What is called an acute knowledge of human nature is mostly nothing but the observer's own weaknesses reflected back from others.

8

He who knows himself properly can very soon learn to know all other men. It is all reflection.

9

I said to myself: *I cannot possibly believe that*, and as I was saying it I noticed I had already believed it a second time.

10

Men who know well how to observe themselves and are secretly proud of it often rejoice at the discovery of a weakness in themselves when the discovery ought to disturb them. That much higher do many rate the professor over the man.

11

It is a fault common to all people of little talent and more reading than understanding that they hit upon ingenious rather than natural explanations.

12

There are faces in the world one absolutely cannot call *Du*.

13

Is it not strange that we should always regard the public that praises us as a competent judge, while as soon as it finds fault with us we declare it incapable of passing judgement on things of the spirit?

14

It is a pity we cannot see the learned entrails of a writer so as to discover what he has eaten.

15

When we ask what the time is we are not seeking to know how the watch is constituted ... Knowledge of means without any actual application of them, without indeed any talent for applying them or any will to do so, is what is nowadays commonly called *erudition*.

16

Since this life is no more than an evanescent point of time, I find it incomprehensible that the state of unending bliss and glory does not begin at once.

17

People find it harder to believe in miracles than in traditions of miracles, and many a Turk, Jew etc., who will now let himself be killed for his tradition would have remained very calm and composed had he been witness to the miracle when it happened . . .

18

There exists a condition which with me at least is not all that rare in which the presence and the absence of a beloved person are equally hard to endure; or at least in which the pleasure derived from their presence is not that which, to judge from the intolerableness of their absence, one would have expected it to be.

19

From the folly of the people in Bedlam it should have been possible to infer more of what man is than has been done hitherto.*

20

Girls possess a certain virginity of the soul and can be morally deflowered, and often are when they are very young indeed.

21

The heroes of the poets of antiquity are very different from those in, e.g., Milton. They are brave, shrewd and wise, but seldom amiable or compassionate in the sense of our morality. Milton took his from the Bible. Does our Christian morality perhaps have its origin in a certain weakness, in a Jewish cowardice, while the other is founded on strength? Universal acceptability is perhaps only a fair chimera and something that will never be attained.

22

Sometimes we know a person better than we can say, or at least than we do say. Words, degree of cheerfulness, mood, indolence, wit, interest – they all lead us to falsity.

23

Where moderation is an error indifference is a crime.

24

To make man as religion wants him to be resembles the undertaking of the Stoics: it is only another grade of the impossible.

25

I have always found that so-called bad people gain in one's estimation when one gets to know them better, and good people decline.

26

He marvelled at the fact that cats had two holes cut in their fur at precisely the spot where their eyes were.

27

How happily many a man would live if he concerned himself with other people's affairs as little as he does with his own.

28

There are people who can believe everything they want to: what fortunate creatures they are!

29

There are very many people who read simply to prevent themselves from thinking.

30

To err is *human* also in so far as animals seldom or never err, or at least only the cleverest of them do so.

31

A great genius will seldom make his *discoveries* on paths frequented by others. When he discovers things he usually also discovers the path to discovery.

32

Popular presentation is today all too often that which puts the mob in a position to talk of something without understanding it.

33

The plain style of writing is to be recommended if only because no honest man takes elaborate pains over what he says.

34

Almost all our writers share the defect of cultivating themselves through other writings and then merely putting them together . . . They read about a thing before they have thought about it, so that in the end their whole knowledge consists of knowing that which others have known.

35

The nightingales sing and have no idea of the fuss poets and lovers create over their song, or that there exists a whole society of higher beings who entertain themselves solely with Philomena and her complaints. Perhaps a higher race of spirits regards our poets as we do canaries and nightingales: they enjoy their song precisely because they find no rational sense in it.

36

To most of the opponents of rhyme there no doubt applies what Dryden said of Milton: they possess no talent for rhyme.

37

The book which most deserved to be banned would be a catalogue of banned books.

38

Because he always neglected his own duties he had time to observe which of his fellow citizens neglected theirs and to report the fact to the authorities.

39

To make other people laugh is no great feat so long as one does not mind whether they are laughing at our wit or at us ourselves.

40

If someone left 100,000 Louis d'or to the greatest rogue in Germany, how many claimants there would be to the legacy!

41

Among the greatest discoveries human reason has made in recent times is, in my opinion, the art of reviewing books without having read them.

42

The American who first discovered Columbus made a bad discovery.

43

He had lived with her for some years in the state of unholy matrimony.

44

She is not yet married, to be sure, but she has taken her doctorate.

45

To shake your head when saying Yes and to nod it when saying No is a hard thing to do, but it acquires a meaning of its own when you can do it.

46

The human tendency to regard little things as important has produced very many great things.

1784–1788

1

The noble simplicity in the works of nature only too often originates in the noble shortsightedness of him who observes it.

2

Among those things that have most made me smile is the idea entertained by certain missionaries of baptizing a whole yardful of proselytes with a fire-engine . . .

3

There is a great difference between believing something and being unable to believe its opposite. I can very often believe something without being able to prove it, just as I do not believe something without being able to refute it. The stance I adopt will be determined not by strict proof but by preponderance of evidence.

4

If you reflect on the history of philosophy and natural science you will find that the greatest discoveries have been made by people who have regarded as merely probable that which others have propagated as certain; that is to say by the adherents of the New Academy who maintained a mid-course between the rigorous certainty of the Stoic and the uncertainty and indifference of the Sceptic. Such a philosophy is the more to be recommended in that we accumulate our opinions at an age when our understanding is at its weakest. This last deserves to be taken into account with regard to religion.

5

I believe the surest way of promoting the progress of mankind would be through the civilizing of the natural talents of the barbarian (who stands between the savage and the civilized man) by means of philosophy communicated by the polished reason of the civilized man. If the savage and the barbarian should ever vanish from the world it will be all up with us.

6

We can do good in as many ways as we can sin, in thought, word and deed.

7

The most dangerous untruths are truths slightly distorted.

8

We have to believe that everything has a cause, as the spider spins its web in order to catch flies. But it does this before it knows there are such things as flies.

9

There are truths which go around so dressed up you would take them for lies, but which are pure truths none the less.

10

He who is enamoured of himself will at least have the advantage of being inconvenienced by few rivals.

11

An imaginary incapacity can with timid people long play the role of a real one, in works of the head just as much as of the body.

12

Because people have such a strong tendency to put things off and take things slowly, so that what ought to happen at five in the morning commonly takes place at six, you can count for certain on retaining the upper hand in any matter if you do everything without the slightest delay.

13

Virtue by premeditation isn't worth much. Feeling or habit is the thing.

14

Many people reveal a gift for pretending to be stupid before they are wise; girls very often possess this gift.

15

Servant-girls kiss children and shake them vigorously when they are observed by a man; they present them quietly, on the other hand, when women are looking on.

16

Man is capable of his greatest works when his mental powers are already on the wane, just as it is hotter in July at two in the afternoon, when the sun is already declining, than it is in June at midday.

17

On education we should not indulge in abstract reasoning, but first assemble the results of experience as to which nation has produced the greatest, most active people; not the greatest compilers and authors, but the most steadfast, the most magnanimous, the most skilful in the arts, etc. – But that will probably be the English.

18

Kings often believe that what their generals and admirals do is done out of patriotism and zeal for their own honour. But the whole motivation of great deeds is more often a girl who reads the newspapers.

19

If a traveller arrived on a remote island and encountered a people whose houses were all hung with loaded rifles and who mounted guard on them all night, what else could he think but that the whole island was inhabited by robbers? But are things any different with the nations of Europe? . . .

20

Just as there are polysyllabic words that say very little, so there are also monosyllabic words of infinite meaning.

21

It is a great trick of oratory sometimes merely to persuade people when you could have convinced them; then they will often think they have been convinced when in fact all you are able to do is merely persuade them.

22

Nothing arouses the curiosity of youth more than fragments of useful knowledge interwoven into pleasing poetry. Thomson's *Seasons* is a masterpiece in this, and must have awoken a love of nature in many an Englishman.

23

With prophecies the commentator is often a more important man than the prophet.

24

One begets the idea, another is godfather at its baptism, the third begets children by it, the fourth visits it on its deathbed, and the fifth buries it.

25

Not only did he not believe in ghosts, he wasn't even afraid of them.

26

He could say the word 'succulent' in such a way that when you heard it you thought you were biting into a ripe peach.

27

Once he has stolen his 100,000 talers a rogue can walk through the world an honest man.

28

It is very charming to hear a foreign woman speak our language and make mistakes with her fair lips. Not so in the case of men.

29

Is it not strange that the rulers of the human race should be so much superior in rank to its teachers? In this we see what a slavish animal man is.

30

There was a time in Rome when they reared fishes with more care than they did children. In our case it is horses . . .

31

If the world should endure for an incalculable number of years the universal religion will be a purified Spinozism. Left to itself, reason can lead to nothing else and it is impossible that it ever will lead to anything else.

32

Our false philosophy is incorporated in our entire language; we can, so to speak, not reason without reasoning falsely. We fail to consider that speaking, regardless of what, is a philosophy . . . Our whole philosophy is rectification of colloquial linguistic usage, thus rectification of a philosophy, and indeed of the most universal and general . . .

33

However we may imagine the nature of the things outside us to be, something of the subject will and must always adhere to them. It is, it seems to me, a very unphilosophical idea to regard our soul as a merely passive thing; no, it also lends to the objects. In this way there can be no creature in the world which knows the world as it is . . .

34

One cannot too often reflect that *the existence of a God, the immortality of the soul*, and the like are things merely *conceivable*, not *perceptible*. They are combinations of ideas, thought-games, to which nothing objective needs to correspond . . .

35

To say we perceive *external* objects is contradictory; it is impossible for man to go outside himself. When we believe we are seeing objects we are seeing only ourselves. We can really perceive nothing in the world except ourselves and the changes that take place in us. It is likewise impossible for us to *feel* for others, as it is customary to say we do; we feel only for ourselves. The proposition sounds a harsh one, but it is not when it is correctly understood. We love neither father, nor mother, nor wife, nor child: what we love are the pleasant sensations they produce in us . . . Nothing else is at all possible, and he who denies this proposition cannot have understood it . . .

36

Rational free-spirits are the light brigade who go on ahead and reconnoitre the ground which the heavy brigade of the orthodox will eventually occupy.

37

The ass seems to me like the horse translated into Dutch.

38

What am I? What shall I do? What can I believe and hope for? Everything in philosophy can be reduced to this . . .

39

It would I think be very much worthwhile for once *truly* to investigate why it is we know *nothing* of the origin of motion . . . A more definite limit exists here than elsewhere, because it seems to be not so much a lack of knowledge as an *absolute barrier*, or at least an indication as to where such a barrier is to be sought.

40

Has anyone ever investigated why the noses of healthy dogs are so wet? The intention could easily be that many odours are more easily precipitated upon it.

Winter 1789

1

Honour is infinitely more valuable than positions of honour.

2

Let's let the grass grow over it.

3

Where we experience no localized sensation, where we do not actually feel an impression on our organs of sense, we cannot reduce anything to bodily effects. If we were unable to close our eyes we would not know whether we see with our head or with our belly . . .

4

If the New Testament faithfully transmits the precepts of the Christian religion then the Catholic religion is hardly Christian . . . The Catholic religion received its present form during ages of the grossest ignorance; it is impossible for a man again permitted to employ his reason to continue to adhere to it – it can be maintained only by fire and sword.

5

The thoughts written on the walls of madhouses by their inmates might be worth publicizing.

6

Snuff is smuggled out of France into Spain and out of Spain into France.

7

Reviews are by absolutely no means judgements of God.

8

If another Messiah was born he could hardly do so much good as the printing-press.

9

To discover relationships and similarities between things that no one else sees. Wit can in this way lead to invention.

1789–1793

1

It makes your hair stand on end when you reflect on how much time and effort has been expended on the elucidation of the Bible . . . And what, after centuries or millennia, will in the end have been gained through these exertions? Certainly nothing more than the knowledge that, like all books, the Bible is a book written by men. By men who, because they lived in somewhat different times, were somewhat different from us; who were somewhat simpler than we are, but on the other hand also very much more ignorant; that the Bible is thus a book containing much that is true and much that is false, much that is good and much that is bad. The more an elucidation of the Bible shows it to be a quite ordinary book the better that elucidation is . . .

2

Writing is an excellent means of awakening in every man the system slumbering within him; and everyone who has ever written will have discovered that writing always awakens something which, though it lay within us, we failed clearly to recognize before.

3

Why does a suppurating lung give so little warning and a sore on the finger so much?

4

The construction of the universe is certainly very much easier to explain than is that of a plant . . .

5

Although I know, of course, that very many reviewers do not read the books they review in so exemplary a way, I none the less cannot see what harm it could do if one were to read a book one is intending to review.

6

I read somewhere – in Rousseau's *Emile*, if I am not mistaken – that a man who rose every day with the sun and went to bed when it set is supposed to have lived to be over a hundred. I believe, however, that where *one* such instance of orderly behaviour is encountered in a man others are to be inferred, and it is these that may be responsible for his age.

7

What would have happened to Luther today? He would have been taken to Spandau, that's for sure.

8

Bavaria, says the king, is a paradise inhabited by animals (he should have said beasts).

9

One use of dreams is that, unprejudiced by our often forced and artificial reflections, they represent the impartial outcome of our entire being. This thought deserves to be taken very much to heart.

10

A schoolteacher or professor cannot educate individuals, he educates only species. A thought that deserves taking to heart.

11

I believe that instinct in man can forestall reason, and that much may therefore be revealed to a less instructed but more acute sensibility that reason has as yet been unable to pursue or attain . . . I include in this the doctrine of the immortality of the soul. After our life is over things will be as they were before it began: this is an instinctive anticipation of any conclusion of reason. It cannot be proved, but for me it possesses, taken together with other conditions such as states of unconsciousness or stupefaction, an irresistible force, and presumably does so too for a host of people who do not want to admit it. Not one argument of reason has yet convinced me otherwise. My view in this matter is nature, the latter is an *art* the product of which everything contradicts as wholly and completely as anything can be contradicted.

12

The only significant thing about the *Histoire secrete* of Mirabeau is that it was printed. All men treat themselves in this way in private . . .

13

Do you believe the world has ever been any different from what it is now? Do you believe blackthorn bushes have ever borne oranges? No. Very well, do you believe, then, that there have ever been men who were sons of God? Yes! O thou just God, how far thy gift of reason can sink! What a poor instrument reason is.

14

When he goes to church and reads his Bible the ordinary man confuses the means with the end. N.B. a very common error.

15

Mathematics has its independence of everything that is not mere quantity solely to thank for the great advances that have been made in it. Everything that is not quantity is thus completely alien to it. Since, therefore, it is concerned with this alone and, being nothing but the development of the laws of the human mind, requires no outside assistance, it is not only the most certain and dependable of all the human sciences but also certainly the *easiest*. Everything that can serve its enlargement resides in man himself. Nature equips every intelligent man with the complete apparatus; we receive it as our endowment. It is the easiest of all sciences in as much as we cannot ever hope to progress as far in any other. For he who can prove the 47th proposition in the first book of Euclid has already made much more progress in the development of these laws of the human mind or of quantity than anyone has ever made in physics.

16

The very fact that so many writers take the trouble to emphasize the humanity of Frederick the Great is a stronger indication than all the praise of his panegyrists that they have taken him for something superhuman which they seek with their censure not so much to denigrate as to equate with what is usually merely called a great man.

17

The Catholics once burned the Jews and failed to reflect that the mother of God was of that nation, and even now do not reflect that they worship a Jewess.

18

I have enjoyed his company in the way the healthy enjoy their health, simply by happily partaking of it, and I perceived its value only after I began to lose it.

19

I forget most of what I have read, just as I do most of what I have eaten, but I know that both contribute no less to the conservation of my mind and my body on that account.

20

Alas, he exclaimed when things went wrong, if only I had done something pleasantly wicked this morning I would at least know why I am suffering now!

21

Twice as much port is certainly drunk in England in a year as is grown in Portugal.

22

If brandy was made out of sparrows there would soon be no sparrows.

23

With our wretched education, as a result of which we are obliged to forget again in the second half of our life what we have learned in the first, it requires effort to write simply, so that in the end we believe that everything that requires effort is simple and good.

24

When in a dream I dispute with someone and he contradicts and instructs me it is I who am instructing myself, *that is to say reflecting*.

This reflection thus presents itself in the form of conversation. Can we be surprised, therefore, if earlier peoples expressed their thoughts about the serpent (as with Eve) with: *the serpent spoke to me*. The Lord spoke to me. My spirit spoke to me. Since we *do not know where* we think, we can remove our thoughts to wherever we wish. Just as we can speak so that he who hears us believes the voice is coming from a third person, so we can think, too, as though we were being spoken to. *Genius Sokratis*, etc. What an astonishing amount may we not yet learn from dreams.

25

Everything the man said possessed its own peculiar weightiness. He was not always capable of descending to the common man's level of comprehension, and even those well versed in him often found his maxims as hard to grasp at first as they found them hard to forget once they had grasped them.

26

In Göttingen we live in funeral pyres furnished with doors and windows.

27

In regard to the body there are if not more then as many who are sick in imagination as are sick in reality, in regard to the mind as many if not very many more who are healthy in imagination as are really healthy.

28

If they took people at the pawnshop I wonder how much I would get for myself. Debtors' prisons are really pawnshops in which money is lent not so much on goods as on the possessors of them.

— 29

How might letters be most efficiently copied so that the blind might read them with their fingers?

30

The true function of the writer in relation to mankind is continually to *say* what most men think or feel without realizing it. Mediocre writers say only what everyone would have *said* . . .

31

If walking on two legs is not natural to man it is certainly an invention that does him credit.

32

God said: Thou shalt not steal – that is more effective than any demonstration of the harmfulness of stealing . . .

33

Enlightenment in all classes of society really consists in *correctly grasping what our essential needs are.*

34

Overwiseness is one of the most contemptible kinds of unwisdom.

35

During my nervous illness I very often found that that which usually offended only my moral feeling now overflowed into the physical. When Dieterich said one day: God strike me dead! I felt so ill I had to forbid him my room for a time.*

36

Relative to the subject an idea is sensation, to the *immediate* object perception.

37

Revelation does not make me understand a thing, it makes me understand it when it is founded on authority. But what authority can constrain me to believe something that contradicts my reason? Only the word of God. But do we possess any word of God that stands outside reason? Certainly not. For it is men who have said that the Bible is the word of God, and men can know no word of God other than reason.

38

It was no friendly act on the part of Herr Kant towards his readers to have written his works in such a fashion that they have to be studied like a work of nature. With works of nature the zeal and effort involved in their investigation is sustained by the conviction that the whole is worth investigating and that if one discovers anything it will be something worthy of the effort one has expended. In the case of the works of man, however, this is not to be expected, for it may be that their author has gone astray and all will in the end eventuate in a Jacob-Böhmism . . . The subjects Herr Kant treats of in his book are very interesting, to be sure, but not everyone is to know that.

39

Long before the invention of the Papacy and Purgatory it was already a common practice to pray for the dead . . . It is nothing more than the humanization, the making humane, of all that of which we know and can know nothing that we encounter everywhere.

40

Can it be that the evil in the world is in general of more use than the good?

41

Many are obscurely aware of how mechanical man is in all his so-called acts of free will . . . In regard to the body we are quite obviously slaves . . . What if belief we are acting freely consists merely in the feeling that now the clock is working properly?

42

However did men arrive at the concept of *freedom*? It was a great idea.

43

Our theologians want to make of the Bible a book in which there is no *human* understanding.

44

That a false hypothesis is sometimes to be preferred to the correct one can be seen in the case of the doctrine of the freedom of man. Man is certainly not free, but not to be misled by this idea requires a very profound study of philosophy ... Freedom is thus really the most convenient and comfortable way of picturing the matter to oneself and, since it has appearance so very much on its side, will for all time remain the most usual one.

45

In the eyes of God there are only rules, strictly speaking only one rule with no exceptions. Because we do not know this supreme rule we construct general rules which are not rules at all; it could well be possible, indeed, that what we call rules could even for finite beings constitute exceptions.

46

Belief in a God is instinct, as natural to man as walking on two legs; in many it is modified, to be sure, and in many even stifled altogther. In the normal way it is present and, if the faculty of perception, our inner being, is to be well formed and balanced, indispensable.

47

To know how to employ the unexpected occurrences of life to one's own advantage in such a way that people believe you have foreseen and desired them is often called being fortunate and is the making of a man in the world. Indeed, merely to know this rule and to keep it always in mind is itself a strength and support. In the opinion of La Rochefoucauld, Cardinal de Retz possessed this quality to a high degree.

48

If only I had passed the point of separation. My God, how I long for the moment when for me time will cease to be time, in the womb of the maternal all and nothing in which I was sleeping when the Hainberg was deposited, when Epicurus, Caesar, Lucretius lived and wrote and Spinoza thought the greatest thought that has ever come into a human head.

49

I believe from the bottom of my soul and after the most mature reflection that the teaching of Christ, cleansed of the accursed scribblings of priests and suitably adapted to our mode of expression, is the most perfect system that I at least can conceive of for the promotion of peace and happiness in the world in the speediest, most vigorous, most certain and most universal way. I also believe, however, that there is another system proceeding wholly from pure reason and leading to the same result, but it is only for practised thinkers and not at all for men in general; and even if it found general understanding the teaching of Christ would none the less have to be preferred for practical application. At the same time Christ submitted to matter, and this compels the admiration even of the atheist. (Every thinker will know in what sense I here employ the word atheist.) How easy it would have been for such a mind to think up a system of pure reason which would have completely satisfied all philosophers. But where were the men for it? Centuries might have elapsed in which no one would have understood it, and was such a thing as that supposed to serve to guide and lead the human race and sustain it in the hour of death? What, indeed, would the Jesuits of all ages and nations not have made out of it? That which is to guide men must be true but also universally understandable. Even if it is presented to them in images which they elucidate differently at each different stage on the road to knowledge.

50
Pain warns us not to exert our limbs to the point of breaking them. How much knowledge would we not need to recognize this by the exercise of mere reason . . .

51
To the back of his head he had fastened a false pigtail, and to the front a pious countenance that was not much more genuine . . .

52
Use, use your powers: what now costs you effort will in the end become mechanical.

53
I do not believe it wholly impossible that a man might live for ever, for continual diminution does not necessarily imply cessation.

54

In England the booksellers call the big folios *tombstones*.

55

In an English women's political club it was laid down as a rule that on important occasions except for the chairwoman only two people were to be permitted to speak at the same time.

56

This is still the soft reverberation of a heavy thunderclap of superstition (conscience, etc.).

57

Since we possess the Bible, the most useless writings of our time seem to be the moralistic – one might almost be inclined to borrow the declaration of the Calif Omar at the burning of the library at Alexandria and say: Either they contain what already stands in the Bible, in which case they are useless, or they are against it, in which case they must be burned. Most of our moralistic writings are really no more than embroideries on the Ten Commandments.

58

There are, to be sure, many upright Christians, there is no question about that, just as there are good men everywhere and in all classes; but this much is certain, that *in corpore* and whatever they have undertaken as such has never been worth very much.

59

Herr Levaillant ramarks in his *Travels in the Interior of Africa*, p. 299, that eagles also eat carrion, and he begs the poets of ancient and modern times to forgive him for so greatly degrading the proud bird of Jupiter. He adds, however, that the eagle does so only in case of necessity, and what does one not do in case of necessity? The eagle thus does what his poets would also do if the necessity arose: he goes along with the times. Jupiter himself, indeed, strove to win the approbation of Europa behind a mask in which he retained of his former splendour only – the horns. It is behind the same mask that a proud author is now striving for the approbation of Germania, and he seems to be succeeding in gaining it.

60

This entire doctrine is worthless except as a subject of dispute.

61

Non cogitant, ergo non sunt.

62

A post-mortem examination cannot uncover those faults which end with death.

63

That is the weather-side of my moral constitution: I can withstand something on that side.

64

I have drawn his picture so that he will find it easier to recover his body on the Last Day.

65

A great speech is easy to learn by heart and a great poem even easier. How hard it would be to memorize as many words linked together senselessly, or a speech in a foreign tongue! Sense and understanding thus come to the aid of memory. Sense is order and order is in the last resort conformity with our nature. When we speak rationally we are only speaking in accordance with the nature of our being. That is why to annex something to our memory we always seek to introduce sense or some other kind of order into it. That is why we devise genera and species in the case of plants and animals. The hypotheses we make belong here too: we are obliged to have them because otherwise we would be unable to retain things . . . The question is, however, whether everything is legible to us. Certainly experiment and reflection enable us to introduce a significance into what is not legible, either to us or at all: thus we see faces or landscapes in the sand, though they are certainly not there. The introduction of symmetries belongs here too, silhouettes in inkblots, etc. Likewise the gradation we establish in the order of creatures: all this is *not in the things but in us*. In general we cannot remember too often that when we observe nature, and especially the ordering of nature, it is always ourselves alone we are observing.

66

When Franklin died they should have hung crape on all the lightning-conductors.*

67

One Pope (Zacharias, I believe) excommunicated people who believed in the antipodes, and now it could easily happen that a Pope could one day excommunicate the antipodes if they fail to believe in the infallibility of their Roman antipodes . . .

68

When in bed with his wife he very much liked to lie antipodally, à l'antipode.

69

It is and always will be a strange expression to say 'The soul is in me, it is in the body', when we should say 'I am this' – for we do not say 'the roundness is in the sphere'. It is merely analogy that misleads us here. Similarity is something objective, but analogy is subjective.

70

The fly that does not want to be swatted is safest if it sits on the fly-swat.

71

Rousseau says: a child who learns to know only its parents does not know even them. Very fine and true.

72

If we think much for ourselves we discover that much wisdom has been gathered into language. It is not very probable that we ourselves carry it all in, but much wisdom does in fact reside there, as it does in proverbs.

73

What she accounted virtue was, as I believe Crébillon says, rather the repenting of sins than the avoidance of them.

74

Westminster Abbey will one day be called *the Golgotha of sculpture*.

75

Sometimes I was in no condition to say whether I was sick or well.

76

Fontenelle was once asked how it came about that he had so many friends and no enemies: *Par ces deux axiomes*, he replied, *tout est possible, et tout le monde a raison*.

77

I believe that, just as the adherents of Herr Kant always accuse their opponents of not understanding him, so there are many who believe Herr Kant is right because they do understand him. His mode of exposition is novel and differs greatly from the usual one, and once we have finally succeeded in understanding it there is a great temptation to regard it as true, especially as he has so many zealous adherents; we ought always to remember, however, that the fact that we understand it is in fact no reason for regarding it as true. I believe that delight at having understood a very abstract and obscure system leads most people to believe in the truth of what it demonstrates.

78

It would be strange if the true system of philosophy and the true system of the cosmos both came out of Prussia . . .

79

Nothing is more common than for people to consider themselves convinced of the truth of a thing once they have understood the view of it a great man has harboured . . . I believe that many a man, once he has worked his way through the difficulties of the Tychonian system and all its epicycles, has thought: 'praise be to God, now I have finally got it all clear.'

80

The best way of praising the living and the dead is to excuse their failings and to apply all one's knowledge of human nature in doing so.

But do not invent virtues they did not possess: that ruins everything and casts doubt even on the truth. Exculpation of faults commends the panegyrist.

81

The celebrated miser John Elwes used to say: If you keep one servant you will have all your work done, if you keep two only half of it, and if you keep three you will have to do it yourself.

82

I have gone down the road to science in the way dogs go for a walk with their masters, backwards and forwards along it a hundred times, and when I arrived I was tired.

83

According to the London tables of mortalities, more people kill themselves than kill other people. In London 539 have been murdered over 75 years: 2,869 have murdered themselves. According to the same tables, 139,248 died of old age. It is nice to see that roughly as many die of old age as die of the pox: so that old age is thus one of the commonest and at the same time most dangerous illnesses afflicting mankind. And not everyone who catches the pox dies of it, while everyone who catches the latter dies of it. Almost twice as many murder themselves as die of side-stitch. At least old age is not a contagious illness, *or* if old age is an illness it is contagious in many families.

84

Health is contagious.

85

One cannot demand of a scholar that he show himself a scholar everywhere in society, but the whole tenor of his behaviour must none the less betray the thinker, he must always be instructive, his way of judging a thing must even in the smallest matters be such that people can see what it will amount to when, quietly and self-collected, he puts this power to scholarly use.

86

Such people do not really defend Christianity, but they do let Christianity defend them.

87

He had learned to play a couple of little pieces on the keyboard of metaphysics.

88

Mississippi: a word with eleven letters and yet only four – four s, four i, two p and an m.

89

Anyone who plunders an idea from a writer of antiquity could defend himself by appealing to metempsychosis and say: prove I was not also that writer.

90

In the writings of celebrated authors but mediocre brains we find at the most only what they want to show us, whereas in the writings of the systematic thinker who mentally embraces everything we see the whole and how everything hangs together. The former seek and find their needle by the light of a sulphur-match which casts a light, and that dimly, only on the place where it happens to be, whereas the latter ignite a candle that floods everything with light.

91

We cannot truly know whether we are not at this moment sitting in a madhouse.

92

Most propagators of a faith defend their propositions, not because they are convinced of their truth, but because they once asserted they were true.

93

To the fame of the most celebrated men there always appertains something of the blinkered foolishness of their admirers, and I am convinced that an awareness that some people possessing less fame but more intelligence can see through them mars all their fame for such men. Genuine serenity in the enjoyment of life is compatible only with truth. Newton, Franklin: they were really to be envied.

94

Nothing offers me such clear proof of how things stand in the world of learning than the circumstance that Spinoza was for so long regarded as an evil, worthless person and his opinions as dangerous; the fame of so many others has suffered a like fate.

95

Twenty years ago I lived opposite an open square that lay between two parallel streets and was paved only at the edge. When it happened that anyone – but here it would be a good idea first to draw a sketch, and for the sake of brevity merely in our head. Imagine a square whose four corners I will designate A B C D, with A and B indicating the two upper corners and C and D the lower ones, A being opposite to D and B opposite to C. When it happened, I say, that someone wanted to cross from D to A or from C to B, or the reverse – which might easily happen 500 times a day – this is how they would do it. When the weather was fine people crossed as nearly as they could along the diagonal. When the weather was bad, or when the unpaved part of the square was very muddy, instead of the diagonal they chose the two sides, at the same time usually looking across at the opposite corner before setting out on this journey and increasing their pace a little. As the unpaved ground became drier, bolder spirits or those who cared less for their shoes no longer walked completely round the corner but crossed over along paths that ran parallel to the diagonal; these paths gradually approached more and more closely to the diagonal, and thus for the most part it continued. Occasionally, however, a vigorous traveller who had already endured a foul road outside the town, or people whose shoes and stockings could hardly be dirtier than they were or who possessed neither the one nor the other, would shorten the whole process. But the most noteworthy phenomenon occurred on mornings when there had been a heavy snowfall the night before. As soon as day dawned I discovered a varying number of individual footprints which were supposed to follow the direction of the diagonal but which in fact followed neither that direction nor any other simple direction in the world. Often they lay along a crooked line which you could bet two to one was not an eighth shorter than the two sides of the parallelogram, and the whole world to a halfpenny was not a thousandth more comfortable (wrong). By eight o'clock the footprints were already joined together to form a pathway, and before it struck eleven you could see very wise and sober men who were certainly aware that the shortest way from one corner of a parallelogram to the opposite corner is the diagonal following with grave and steady step a crooked line which perhaps a sleepy nightwatchman had taken for the diagonal. This was at first a narrow path, but then many people came along who usually shared it with one another so politely that none was actually walking on it, and in this way it grew wider . . .

96

In the end everything comes down to the question: does thought originate in feeling or feeling in thought? . . . This is the ultimate principle of religion, and the answer to the question 'is the power of feeling or the power of thought the ultimate reality?' draws the final frontier between theism and atheism.

97

After a Thirty Years War with himself peace was at last concluded: but the time was lost to him.

98

It always saddens me when a man of talent dies, for the earth has more need of such men than Heaven does.

99

There are so-called mathematicians who would like to be regarded as emissaries of wisdom with just as much fervour as many theologians would like to be regarded as emissaries of God, and who impose just as much upon the people with the algebraical rigmarole they call mathematics as do the latter with a gibberish upon which they confer the name Biblical.

100

To express truly what one has truly felt – that is to say with those little expressive traits that testify one is speaking of one's own experience – is what really makes the great writer: ordinary writers always avail themselves of phrases and expressions that are nothing but clothes from the second-hand market.

101

Boorishness, too, has its geniuses, and who will call nature to account for having proclaimed this gift to its possessor through the flattering feeling of strength and superiority and self-contentment? The ways of Heaven are dark and devious and its comforts manifold.

102

Resolved: to send out arrest-warrants when someone has borrowed an idea from me and then appropriated it.

103

The idea we have of a soul has much in common with that of a magnet under the earth. It is merely an image. To picture everything in such forms as this is an inborn inventive faculty in man.

104

In the preface to the second and third edition of Kant's *Critique* (the third is only a reprint of the second) many singular things appear that I have often thought but never said. We discover no cause in things but notice only that which corresponds to something within ourselves. Wherever we look we see only ourselves.

105

Oh the girl was a Bethesda, and I always came too late.

106

A creature of a higher kind makes the whole history of the world repeat itself, in the way one makes a watch repeat.

107

The course of the seasons is a clock in which a cuckoo goes 'cuckoo' when spring arrives.

108

Is it not strange that in all his writings Lord Chancellor Bacon never once refers to the great Roger Bacon (Friar Bacon), since he was not only his namesake but a fellow of his own faculty? William Jones says, in his *Physiological Disquisitions*, Introd. p. xxv, that he had been assured of this fact by a man who had gone through Bacon's works solely with a view to establishing it.

109

A father says: The accursed boy does exactly as I do, I'll beat him until he doesn't know what day it is.

110

He was able to divide up an idea everyone thought simple into seven other ideas as a prism divides up a ray of sunlight, each idea more beautiful than the last, and then again collect together a host of other ideas and produce a ray of white sunlight where others saw only many-coloured confusion.

111
Epitaph at Arlington, near Paris

> Here lie
> Two grandmothers with their two granddaughters
> Two husbands with their two wives
> Two fathers with their two daughters
> Two mothers with their two sons
> Two maidens with their two mothers
> Two sisters with their two brothers.
> Yet but six corpses all lie buried here,
> All born legitimate, from incest clear.

This riddle, which was given to me by someone who himself did not know how to solve it, I read as follows: Two old men each of whom has a grown-up son each of whom has an unmarried daughter marry two young girls who are sisters. After the wedding, however, the two old men are ill and die before the marriages are consummated. After their deaths the two young men marry their stepmothers: these six last are those who lie buried here. For here two sisters are also lying with their two brothers, because every woman calls her sister's husband her brother.

112

It is small consolation if the lack of correspondence between the inner and the outer man, between the esoteric and exoteric, leads us to infer the existence of something similar in the works of nature. For how many friends would remain friends if they could see one another's dispositions as they are as a whole?

113

It is a very prudent arrangement on the part of our nature that we are completely insensible of many extremely dangerous illnesses. If we were aware of apoplexy from its very beginnings onwards it would be counted among the chronic illnesses.

114

Perhaps the roof-tiler fortifies himself to meet the perils of the day through a morning prayer, and if so he is among the fortunate; perhaps, however, he does it with a portion of baked cat's brains. Oh if only we sometimes knew what gives people courage!

115

The most perfect ape cannot draw an ape; only man can do that; but, likewise, only man regards the ability to do this as a sign of superiority.

116

A character: of all things to see only the worst, to fear everything, to regard even health as a condition in which one is unaware of one's illnesses; I believe I could achieve no character better than I could this one.

117

To act absolutely in opposition to one's inclinations is certain in the end to lead to something better. E.g. my drinking nothing at all with meals.

118

I have long thought that philosophy will yet eat up itself. – Metaphysics has eaten up part of itself already.

119

Apologizing for mistakes is all very well as far as it goes, but it usually contributes as little towards correcting one's blunder as when at skittles you try to assist the ball by moving your head, shoulders, arms and legs after it has left your hand: it is more a desire to influence than actual influence.

120

A man who owes his entire reputation to the desire of men to read something bad about their acquaintances.

121

Let us let the grass grow over it.

122

I have made it my rule that the rising sun should never find me in bed so long as I am well. This rule cost me nothing but the making of it, for my attitude towards laws I have imposed upon myself has always been never to impose them until I would find it almost impossible to transgress them.

123

For several days (since 22 April 91) I have lived in accordance with the hypothesis (for I live all the time in accordance with some hypothesis) that *drinking with meals is harmful*, and I feel excellent as a result. There is certainly something true in this. For no change in my way of living, and no medicine, has ever before produced a good effect so quickly or palpably as this has.

124

I have thought a great deal, I know, much more than I have read; as a consequence I am ignorant of a great deal that the rest of the world knows, so that when I mix with the rest of the world I often err and blunder, and this makes me shy and retiring. If I could express all that

I have accumulated in thought, not in a fragmentary and often unattractive way, but as it exists within me, it would certainly receive the world's applause.

125

Only the egoist and the idealist doubt the existence of beings *praeter nos*. But that we transform *praeter* into *extra*, and regard beings *praeter nos* as *extra nos*, think of them as occupying a different space, appears to be a form of our sensitive faculty. But could the *praeter me* not also be a form of our faculty of perception?

126

One of the most telling observations in favour of Kant's theory of space has to me always been the fact that we are obliged to regard physical bodies as being infinitely divisible, which is contradictory to reason; for it is in no way necessary, it is indeed not possible, that e.g. inertia, impenetrability, should be the effect of complex physical bodies, and yet we always imagine these qualities as existing in space. This is the form of sensual perception.

127

A parable: He always wears spurs but never rides.

128

I believe it can be demonstrated with geometrical exactitude that, if the New Testament contains the doctrines of Christianity in their entirety, the Catholic religion cannot in any way be called Christian. Whether any of the Protestant churches are wholly so I leave undecided. I believe you could bet a million to one that, if the question were put to an assembly of the most sensible people of all nations, their decision would be that the Catholic religion resembles the Christian as little as modern Italian does ancient Latin . . .

129

Practical reason or the moral sense: the latter expression will make it clearer to many what one means by the former.

130

Whenever he sees a troup of students, or even only two, riding by, Dieterich always believes his son is among them. It is truly characteristic.

131

I believe we would always bloom and blossom as youth does if we could be always so carefree; or is it, on the contrary, blooming and blossoming that makes one carefree?

132

If Heaven should find it useful and necessary to produce a new edition of me and my life I would like to make a few not superfluous suggestions for this new edition chiefly concerning the design of the frontispiece and the way the work is laid out.

133

It is astonishing how much the word *infinitely* is misused: everything is infinitely more beautiful, infinitely better, etc. The concept must have something pleasing about it, or its misuse could not have become so general.

134

He despises me because he does not know me, and I despise his accusations because I know myself.

135

It was a characteristic of his that he never read bad books but none the less did write them: a sure proof that he had either not understood what he read or must have been unable to grasp the good as it has to be grasped.

136

God himself sees in things only himself.

137

To me there is no more odious kind of person than those who on every occasion believe they are obliged to be *ex officio* witty.

138

In order to find something very many, perhaps most people first have to know it is there.

139

Our forefathers' healthy appetite for food seems now to have been transformed into a not so healthy appetite for reading; and as the Spaniards formerly came running up to watch the Germans eat, so foreigners now come to watch us study.

140

The way we [the different nations of the world] think about the events of life does not differ so widely as does the way we *speak* about them.

141

There are serious illnesses of which we can die; there are, further, those which, though we do not exactly die of them, are none the less very perceptible; finally there are, however, also those which are barely perceptible without a microscope, though when this is applied they too appear truly dreadful: and this microscope is hypochondria. I believe that if men seriously devoted themselves to studying the microscopic diseases they could have the satisfaction of being ill every day.

142

Much has been written about the *first* human beings: someone ought to have a go at writing about the two *last*.

143

'Long live the death of the Protestants,' the Marquis de Langle cried in his *Tableau pittoresque de la Suisse*: he meant that they died with fewer fearful imaginings of Purgatory, etc. It should therefore be: '*Vive la mort dans les pays des protestants*.'

144

Presupposing we do not regard ourselves as an object of observation like a prepared specimen but always as the sum of what we now are, we are lost if we acquire too *much* time for reflecting on ourselves. We become aware of so much that is dismal and wretched that at the sight of it all desire to organize it or hold it together departs from us.

145

A system: Through transmigration of souls every man arrives at the condition which during his life he most desired and envied; thus everything will in the end revolve in a circle and no class be quite empty.

146

It is a question whether, when we break a murderer on the wheel, we do not fall into the error a child makes when it hits the chair it has bumped into.

147

I believe that, in comparison with an Englishman, the German stifles many things with his reason, which is something that ought really never to happen. The German, for example, refrains from laughing because he knows laughter would be improper on many occasions on which it has not so much as occurred to the Englishman to laugh at all.

148

In the preaching of useful truths to men everything is permitted that does not harm or offend anyone: thus fairy tales, too, are permitted. No one any longer finds it absurd when animals speak in fables, so why should it be thought tasteless if it rains pearls? A wise man would *do* more than many a sorcerer in a fairy tale if he could convert a fool to wisdom: why should he not *invent fictions* to that end?

149

He was no 'slave of his word', as the saying goes: on the contrary, he exercised such despotism over his promises he could do with them whatever he liked.

150

We are so constructed it is doubtful if, except on rare occasions, we shall ever be accurate judges of what is useful to us. This is the case in this life; who is to guarantee it is not also the case in regard to the next? Whom the Lord loveth he chastiseth. What if the truth is: whom the Lord loveth he destroyeth?

151

Ought not the King of France be permitted to offer himself for election as a deputy to the National Assembly? It would be better for him.

152

All we really have are transplanters of novels and comedies. Few are raised from seed.

153

You should never look for genuine Christian convictions in a man who makes a parade of his piety.

154

In regard to K.'s taunts and jibes against me and others my greatest comfort, or rather my sweetest revenge, is the perfect conviction that a great and good man would never be capable of them.*

155

'Many are less fortunate than you' may not be a roof to live under, but it will serve to retire beneath in the event of a shower.

156

Many people venture into professions no one expects them to do well in, partly because the public is blinded to defects by its own admiration, and then because the people themselves are less aware of the difficulties of such a profession than they are of those in which they have already engaged.

157

It is said that truth comes from the mouths of fools and children; I wish every good mind which feels an inclination for satire would reflect that the finest satirist always has something of both in him.

158

The form of a game of chess and even that of the Talmud and the old scholastic philosophy are good, but the matter is not of much use. One exercises one's powers, but what one learns in doing so has no value.

159

Many people regard as divine that which has no rational sense in it. Pleasure in contemplating useless algebraic equations one has made up oneself belong in this class.

160

The principle of sufficient reason is, as a purely logical principle, a necessary law of thought, and to this extent it admits of no dispute; whether it is an objective, real, *metaphysical* principle is, however, another question.

161

There is only one plant and only one animal, and these two are one. The animal that lives off plants has its roots in the earth, thus the animal that lives off animals does so too.

162

Every great lord ought to learn an art, as the sultans do: we live in strange times, and you can never know whether you might not need it one day. The previous Turkish emperor was a very good maker of bows and arrows, the present one paints muslin for ladies.

163

Nature has bestowed on the animals sufficient intelligence for them to take care of their self-preservation. They all know very well what to do when it comes to this important matter. Vaillant gives some very good examples of it in the way animals behave at the approach of lions. Nature has almost instinctively armed even man against the fear of death – with the belief in immortality.

164

What Duclos said of Louis XIV can be said of many an author: *Les choix du Roi n'etoient pas toujours approuvés, mais qu'ils etoient toujours applaudis.*

165

The swords that effect the greatest conquests are those encrusted with diamonds.

166

You can make a good living from soothsaying but not from truth-saying.

167

We know with much greater clarity that our will is free than that everything that happens must have a cause. Could we therefore not reverse the argument for once, and say: our conception of cause and effect must be very erroneous because our will could not be free if our idea of cause and effect were correct?

168

As soon as he receives a little applause many a writer believes the world is interested in everything about him. The play-scribbler Kotzebue even thinks himself justified in telling the public that he administered a clister to his dying wife.

169

Moderation presupposes enjoyment, abstemiousness does not. That is why there are more abstemious people than those who enjoy in moderation.

170

S. seldom does wrong, but what he does he usually does at the wrong time.

171

If you give something to three poor people every day, in a year you will have given something to 1,095, and that is an army.

172

Someone read the *Messiade* aloud skipping every other line and the passage was still admired.*

173

There could be an ear to which all the nations were speaking but one language.

174

Two people do not love one another but each would like to make the other love him or her to the point of dying of love or committing suicide: these two write one another letters. The result could be very amusing.

175

Those who first invented the forgiveness of sins through formulas in Latin are guilty of the greatest act of corruption there has ever been.

176

There is something quite natural in the fact that we admire great warriors, as there is in our thirst for conquest: the former corresponds to beauty and bodily strength, the latter to comfort and well-being. It will thus never be possible to philosophize these things out of the world.

177

I regard reviews as a kind of childhood illness to which newborn books are subject to a greater or less degree. There are instances of the soundest dying of them, while the feeble often come through. Many don't catch them at all. Attempts have often been made to ward them off with the aid of the amulets of prefaces and dedications, or even to inoculate them with self-criticisms, but this doesn't always work.

178

One of the most difficult arts for man to acquire is surely the art of acquiring courage. Those who lack it find it most readily under the powerful protection of one who does possess it and who can then aid us if all else fails. Since, however, there is so much affliction in the world against which the courage of no human creature can serve to offer sufficient comfort to the weaker, religion offers an excellent substitute. Religion is really the art of acquiring for oneself comfort and courage in affliction, and the strength to work against it, through thoughts of God and by no other means. I have known people to whom their good fortune was their God. They believed in their good fortune and their belief gave them courage. Courage gave them good fortune and good fortune gave them courage. It is a great loss for a man if he loses his faith in a wise being who directs the world. I believe this is an inevitable consequence of all study of philosophy and of nature. One does not lose belief in a God, to be sure, but it is no longer the benevolent God of our childhood; it is a being whose ways are not our ways and whose thoughts are not our thoughts, and this is not especially helpful to the helpless.

179

If, as Leibniz has prophesied, libraries one day become cities, there will still be dark and dismal streets and alleyways as there are now.

180

They complain at the frightful quantity of bad writing that appears at every Easter fair. I cannot see why they should. Why do the critics say we ought to imitate nature? These writers imitate nature, they follow their instincts just as the great writers do. And I would like to know what more can be asked of any organic being than that it follows its instincts. Look at the trees, I say, for example the cherry-tree, and say how many of the green cherries on it will become ripe: not a fiftieth of them; the rest will fall and decay. But if the cherry-trees produce waste, who shall deny it to men to do so, who are better than the trees? Indeed, why do I talk about trees? Know ye not that of the human beings the procreative public produces every year more than a third die before they are two years old? As with men, so with the books they write. Thus instead of bewailing the rising quantity of scribbling I do reverence rather to the exalted order of nature, whose will it is that of all that is born a greater part shall become manure and waste-paper, which is a kind of manure . . .

181

One of the negro slaves on the plantations of literature.

182

It is strange indeed that long syllables are designated with a ‾ and short ones with a ˇ, since the former is the shortest way between two points and the latter is a crooked line. The inventor of these signs must therefore have been thinking of something else when he invented them, if he was thinking of anything at all.

183

Since a man can go mad I do not see why a universal system cannot do so too . . .

184

In addition to *time* there exists another means of bringing about great changes, and that is – *force*. When the former moves too slowly the latter often anticipates it.

185

Conclusive solution of the riddle in the Taschen-Kalender for 1792. There are two widows, A and B, each of whom has a grown-up son, a and b, and each marries the son of the other: A marries b, and B marries a. Each marriage produces a daughter α and β. These are the six people in the grave.

2 grandmothers with their 2 granddaughters
A and B with α and β
2 husbands with their 2 wives
a and b with A and B
2 fathers with their 2 daughters
a and b with α and β
2 mothers with their 2 sons
A and B with a and b
2 maidens with their 2 mothers
α and β with A and B
2 sisters with their 2 brothers
α with her stepbrother a and β with her stepbrother b.

A justified objection to this solution would be that, if A married b, a would have married his mother's mother-in-law; yet this might well be permitted if, e.g., the marriages took place at the same time, or if a marriage of this kind was not prohibited in England. Incest, however, it is not, and it is only of that that the riddle speaks.

186

The art of making men dissatisfied with their fate so much practised nowadays. Oh if only we could return to the age of the Patriarchs . . . or go to happy Tahiti, where . . . there is perfect human equality and you have the right to eat your enemies and to be eaten by them.

187

The world exists not so that we shall know it but so that we may form ourselves in it. This is a Kantian idea.

188

After having set down many *observations regarding human nature*, and having done so with a flattering sense of my own superiority, and then gone on to refine and improve the wording, I have often discovered in the end that the best I had to say I could simply have written down without any of these sensations just as anyone else might have. (Very, very true.)

189

I was for long unable to understand why it was I found it so fearfully difficult to read the books of many a celebrated polymath, but finally I hit on the answer: the reason is that these people are so insignificant compared with men of true greatness that one cannot summon up the desire to know what it is they know.

190

It is very well said by Herr Schmid in his *Empirical Psychology* that God and immortality are so often called upon to provide comfort and consolation in ordinary everyday affairs that at times when they alone are truly able to offer them they are no longer efficacious.

191

Since the middle of the year 1791 there has arisen in my whole economy of thought something that I cannot yet properly describe. I shall allude to it here only briefly and later pay it more alert attention.

What I mean is an extraordinary distrust, which I have almost been led to commit to writing, of all human knowledge, mathematics alone excepted, and all that still ties me to the study of physics is the hope of discovering something useful to the human race. For we are obliged to think of causes and explanations, because without this endeavour I can see no means at all of keeping ourselves active. It is of course possible to go hunting for weeks on end and shoot nothing, but this much is certain, that we would also have shot nothing if we had stayed at home and, indeed, *certainly* shot nothing, since the possibility of shooting something, however slight it may be, exists only out in the field . . .

192

The roof-tile may know many things the chimney doesn't know.

193

Even the mistakes we so frequently make are useful in that in the end they accustom us to believing that everything may be different from what we imagine it to be. This experience too can, like the seeking after causes, be generalized, so that at last we are bound to arrive at the philosophy which denies even the necessity of the *principii contradictionis*.

194

Given the way we think, the two concepts being and *non-being* are simply impenetrable. For we do not even really know what being is, and as soon as we venture on definition we are obliged to admit that something can exist and be nowhere. Kant also says the same thing somewhere.

195

It is truly astonishing that we have erected our belief in God upon vague ideas of causation. We know nothing of Him, and can know nothing, for to conclude that the world must have a creator is never anything but anthropomorphism.

196

His entire strength lay in being able to give passable expression to what other people had thought.

197

We read so much about genius nowadays everyone believes he is one. The man who early on regards himself as a genius is lost.

198

Is it not strange that Catholic preachers always have to warn their congregations against Protestant writings? Protestant preachers never warn theirs against Catholic ones. If I were a Protestant preacher, indeed, I would, I think, recommend to my congregation the reading of the so-called arch-Catholic books as one of the strongest means of confirming them in their faith.

199

With all my indolence I have ever grown in knowledge of myself without possessing the power to effect an improvement; indeed, the fact that I could perceive how indolent I was has often seemed to me sufficient recompense for it, and the pleasure I received from the exact observation of a fault was often greater than the vexation aroused in me by the fault itself. *So very much more did I account the professor in me than I did the man.* Strange are the ways Heaven directs its saints.

200

Without imagination man would really be nothing at all, for similarity of particulars is in fact the only thing that leads us to scientific knowledge: it is only through similarities that we are able to arrange and retain. The similarities do not reside in the things: in the eyes of God there are no similarities. From which, to be sure, the conclusion must follow that the greater the understanding the more deficient the imagination . . .

201

A golden rule: We must judge men, not by their opinions, but by what these opinions make of them . . .

202

Is a nation entitled to change its political constitution if it wants to? On this question a great deal has been said, both good and bad. I believe the best answer is: Who is to prevent it once it has resolved to do so? . . .

203

This thought was constantly at work in his conscience: surrounded by the bustle of the workaday world he could not hear it, but in the silence of the night he listened to it with all his soul.

204

I have looked at the register of illnesses and did not find anxieties and gloomy thoughts among them: this is very wrong.

205

To dispute badly is better than not to dispute at all. Even the chatter of a pot-house politician makes people wiser – if not about politics, then about other things . . .

206

The tone of voice often determines the assertion, though it is the assertion that should set the tone of voice. Even good writers, if they are also able to speak well, sometimes find they have arrived unawares where they really had no wish to go.

207

Someone described a row of willow-trees planted at a little distance from one another thus: first there stood one tree, then none, then again one and then again none.

208

Instead of saying that the world is reflected in us, we ought rather to say that our reason is reflected in the world. We can do no other than recognize order and judicious direction in the world, but this, however, is a consequence of the structure of our intellect. It does not follow, though, that something we are obliged to think is necessarily really so, for we have no conception at all of the true nature of the external world: from the nature of the external world alone, therefore, it is impossible to demonstrate the existence of God . . .

209

It is a bad thing that truth has nowadays to have its cause pleaded by fiction, novels and fables.

210

It suffices for a man's justification if he has so lived that on account of his virtues he deserves to be forgiven his faults.

211

I watch over the young lady's virtue as though it were my own, says an old governess.

212

Nature has created women as it has so that they shall act not in accordance with principles but in accordance with feeling.

213

That God, or whatever it is, has induced man to propagate himself by making him enjoy coition must also be borne in mind in reflecting on Kant's highest principle of morality.

214

A cares-meter, *mensura curarum*. My face is one.

215

No popery! *Kein Pabst!* Wherever it is, there are popes everywhere.

216

He is another of those who believe man is already finished and complete, so that the Last Day might as well dawn right away.

217

There existed a science of *suprasensible* objects apprehended by reason alone. *Ontology* was a science of *objective* predicates of real objects derived from reason alone which was responsible for the whole metaphysical system. Its chief proposition was the law of contradiction, but this demonstrates nothing but the agreement of an idea with its predicate and not of the idea with the objects.

218

It would perhaps be better for the human race if it were wholly Catholic rather than wholly Protestant. But since Protestantism exists one has to be ashamed to be a Catholic. For the good that came of universal Catholicism has now come to nothing, and to make it universal again is impossible.

219

When in Cochin China someone says *doii* (*doji* = I am hungry), people come running as though there were a fire to give him something to eat. In many a province of Germany a poor man could say *mich hungert* and it would do him as much good as if he said *doii*.

220

It would be a good idea if at the end of each year a tribunal was held on the conduct of the newspapers: perhaps it would make the people who write in them more circumspect . . . Two or more opposing papers would be compared with one another, and all of them with the actual course of events. Thus some assessment of the value of political journals in general would in the end be arrived at . . .

221

People who seal their letters with green sealing-wax are all of a particular kind: usually they are intelligent minds who sometimes themselves engage in chemical experiments and know how difficult it is to make green sealing-wax.

222

We are unwilling to give up false opinions we have conceived of people once we consider ourselves justified in saying they are based on a subtle application of our knowledge of mankind and believe that such insight into the heart of another is possible only to certain initiates. – There are consequently few branches of human knowledge in which a little learning can do more harm than in this branch.

223

People understand loyalty to an upright man much better than they do loyalty to even the best statutes . . .

224

It won't be long before people are classified according to their intellectual abilities as minerals are classified according to their hardness, or actually according to the extent to which each is endowed with the ability to cut and scratch another.

225

We perceive things by means of our senses. But what we perceive is not the things themselves: the eye creates the light and the ear the sounds. Outside of us they do not have these things. We lend them to them. It is just the same with space and time . . .

226

Even if one cannot hew a house out of a granite cliff, one could perhaps hew the *ruins* of a house out of it at no very great expense, so that posterity would be forced to believe a palace had stood there.

227

Formerly when I got annoyed it was with a feeling of strength; now it is with a feeling of passive anxiety.

228

The cultivation of souls, of which brandy-drinking too forms a part, has extinguished many clues through which we might one day have discovered what man originally was and what he ought to have been.

229

If a war has lasted twenty years it can well go on to last a hundred. For war has now become a *status*. Polemocraty. People who have enjoyed peace die out.

230

What kind of beast the soldier is can be seen clearly in the present war. He can be used to uphold freedom or to suppress freedom, to topple kings or to secure them on their thrones. Against France, for France and against Poland!

231

Writers argue against suicide, bringing forward reasons that are supposed to influence our mind at the critical moment. But all this is in vain so long as we have not discovered the reasons for *ourselves*, that is to say if they are not the fruit, the outcome of all our knowledge and of the being we have become. Thus everything calls out to us: strive every day after truth, learn to know the world, devote yourself to acquiring the companionship of honest men, then you will always act as is most beneficial to you; and if one day you should find suicide beneficial, if that is to say all your reasons do not suffice to restrain you from it, then for you suicide too is – permitted.

232

To prevent an effect from occurring at all requires a force equal to the cause of that effect, but to give it a new direction often requires only something very trivial.

233

There are few more unpleasant situations to be in than that of receiving as a gift worthless things upon which however the giver sets an exceptional value and for which he expects no gift in return, though he does expect you to take it. This is the case between me and D. He overwhelms me with so-called delicacies from his table which I am far from regarding as delicacies and which if he were not present I would often give away untouched. And yet I am obliged to hear that he is accustomed to saying that he sometimes gives me food. The honest fellow means nothing but good by it.*

234

My body is that part of the world which my thoughts are able to change. Even *imaginary* illnesses can become real ones. In the rest of the world my hypotheses cannot disturb the order of things.

235

For the loss of those we have loved there is no alleviation but time and carefully and rationally chosen diversions such as will not cause our heart to reproach us.

236

Is it not strange that anyone is permitted to be his own physician or his own lawyer, but as soon as he tries to be his own priest he is greeted with cries and lamentations, in which the gods of the earth too join. Why is it that the gods of the earth are so concerned about the salvation of man in the next world when they are so often irresponsibly neglectful of it in this? The answer is not very difficult.

237

Order leads to all the virtues! but what leads to order?

238

Is the situation so uncommon, then, in which philosophy forbids one to philosophize?

239

They feel the pressure of government as little as they do the pressure of the air.

240

It was clearly noticeable that on the day D. wrote his will and testament he demanded more of me than his politeness usually permitted him to. I could thus perceive that he may well have done something for me or my family on that day. Is it not singular that, without my being able to know anything of the coming reward, he should have imposed upon me things I would not normally have done without recompense, just as though I knew of the reward?

241

France is in fermentation: whether the product will be wine or vinegar is as yet uncertain.

242

To doubt things which are now believed without any further investigation whatever: that is everywhere the main thing.

243

Wherever I experience a new thought, a new theory, always to ask: Is this really as new as you believe it is? This is also in general the best way of remembering never to be amazed at anything in the world (*nil admirari*).

244

Does music make plants grow, or are there among the plants some that are musical?

245

The Spaniards have a proverb: He who wants to become Pope must think of nothing else. Sixtus V followed this prescription.

246

To seek to see in everything something no one has yet seen and no one has yet thought of.

247

To ask in everything the question *Is this true?* by all means – but then to go on to seek grounds for believing it is not true.

248

Nothing is more inimical to the progress of science than the belief that we know what we do not yet know. This is an error to which the inventors of fanciful hypotheses are commonly subject.

249

Man is a masterpiece of creation if for no other reason than that, all the weight of evidence for determinism notwithstanding, he believes he has free will.

250

It is strange that only extraordinary men make those discoveries that afterwards seem so easy and simple; it presupposes that to perceive the simplest but true condition of things requires a very profound degree of knowledge.

251

How do we arrive at the concept of *outside us*? Why do we not believe that everything is *within us* and takes place *within us*? How do we arrive at the concept of distance at all? It is a question that seems very hard to resolve. We go so far as to place that which is within us and takes place within us, namely the changes to the images on our retina, outside us, and yet at once transpose a blow to the eye and the pain that follows it into the eye itself.

252

A man of spirit must not think of the word *difficulty* as so much as existing. Away with it!

253

Outside us. It is truly very hard to say how we arrive at this concept, for what we perceive we really perceive purely within us. To perceive something outside oneself is a contradiction: we perceive only within ourselves, that which we perceive is merely a modification of our self and thus takes place within us. Because these changes do not depend on us ourselves we ascribe them to other things that are outside us and say there exist things – we should say *praeter nos*, but for *praeter* we substitute the preposition *extra*, and that is something quite different. We think of these things as being outside ourselves in space, and that is clearly not perception; it seems to be something most intimately interwoven with the way in which our senses acquire knowledge, it is the form in which that idea of *praeter nos* is presented to us. The form of our sensual faculty.

254

Could our belief that we are acting freely when we are in fact machines not be a form of our understanding? It is altogether impossible for us to observe the act of coming into being, we everywhere observe only what has happened, not how it happens; so that when we believe we are now doing something it has in fact already been done.

255

In the case of sound there exists nothing that corresponds to black in the case of colours. Deathly silence might be called black. An interval is black.

256

Through desultory wanderings on the desultory expeditions of the imagination we quite often put up game which purposeful philosophy can make use of in its well-ordered household.

257

Man is a cause-seeking creature; within the system of spirits he could be called the cause-seeker. Perhaps other spirits conceive of things as being related to one another in ways we would find incomprehensible.

258

A good method of discovery is to imagine certain members of a system removed and then see how what is left would behave: for example, where would we be if iron were absent from the world: this is an old example.

259

Everything the child says and does the man also does, in other matters in which he is and remains a child – for we are all children of more advanced years . . . To be sure, we no longer hit a table we have knocked ourselves against, but we have instead for different but similar knocks devised the word Fate against which we utter accusations.

260

The proper rules for discovering truths are still lacking a Newton and a Herschel.

261

Richter once said to me: physicians should say, not 'I cured him', but 'He did not die at my hands'. In the same way one could also say in physics: I have assigned to it causes whose absurdity no one has yet been able to demonstrate – instead of saying: I have *explained*.

262

Above all things expand the frontiers of science: without this the rest counts for nothing.

263

Do not say hypothesis, and even less theory: say *way of thinking*.

264

Whichever way you look at it, philosophy is always analytical chemistry. The peasant employs all the propositions of the most abstract philosophy, only he employs them enveloped, concealed, compounded, latent, as the chemist and physicist says; the philosopher gives us the propositions pure.

265

In nature we find, not words, but only the initial letters of words, and if we then attempt to read them we find that the new so-called words are again merely the initial letters of other words.

1793–1796

1

What a great achievement it would be to make people do things without knowing they were doing them, in the way that those who love hunting get healthy physical exercise, or he who eats because he is hungry provides nourishment for his body, or he who is really only after pleasure procreates his race . . .

2

Even the best laws can only be respected and feared, not loved. Good rulers are respected, feared and loved. What mighty sources of happiness for a nation good rulers are!

3

The grander and more far-reaching the project of which a revolution is a part, the more suffering the revolution will inflict upon those involved in it: for not everyone is capable of employing his reason for the strengthening of his patience even when he has the whole design in view, and these will be the fewer the more uncertain it is whether they will live to enjoy the fruits. But it is precisely this shortsightedness that prevents even the wisest governments from achieving their great goals by the gentle paths they rightly pursue: for, since it is a natural duty always to choose only what we think good, it is impossible to embark upon a course designed to improve the world but which must in the meantime make millions unhappy. Man is here to cultivate only the surface of the earth: the cultivation and repair that extend further into the depths are reserved by nature for herself. This cultivation has not been entrusted to man. He cannot cause earthquakes that overturn cities, and if he could he would certainly produce them in the wrong place. I am much inclined to believe that the same applies to our *-archies* and *-crasies*. What the plough and the axe can do, that we can and must do, but not what pertains to the earthquake, the flood or the hurricane, though this is probably, indeed certainly, just as useful and necessary.

4

If a higher being were to tell us how the world came into existence I would like to know whether we would be in a position to understand him. I believe not. There would be hardly any mention of the act of coming into existence, for that is mere anthropomorphism. It may even be that outside of our own minds there is nothing at all corresponding to our concept of coming into existence once it is applied, not to relations between things, but to objects in themselves.

5

Much is written nowadays about nomenclature and correct designation, and that is quite right; it must all be worked upon and the best results obtained. Only I believe we expect too much of it and are too anxious to bestow upon things names that are an expression of their nature. The immeasurable advantage which language offers to thinking consists, it seems to me, in its constituting signs for things rather than definitions of them. I believe, indeed, that it is precisely when language is employed as definition that its usefulness is in part annulled. To determine what things are is the task of philosophy. The word should be, not a definition, but merely a sign for the definition that is always the changeable product of the collective labour of researchers; and it will always remain so with regard to such countless objects of our thinking that the thinker will grow accustomed no longer to regarding the sign as a definition and will in the end unconsciously transfer this lack of signification also to those signs that truly are definitions. And this too is, it seems to me, quite right. For, since the signs for concepts cannot be definitions of them, it is almost better to forbid any of them at all to be a definition than for the sake of a few signs that really are definitions to procure a false reputation for all those others which are not. This would create a primacy of language over meaning that would rob us of all the advantages granted us by the signs. But this need not worry us: left to itself, reason will always take words for what they are. Such a defining word accomplishes incredibly little. For a word cannot contain everything, and I therefore still have to get to know the thing itself separately. The best word is one that everybody understands immediately. We must therefore be careful about discarding words that are universally understood, and we should never discard them on the ground that they give a false conception of the thing! For in the first place it is not true that it gives me a false conception, since I of course know and presuppose that the word serves simply to distinguish the thing, and in the second I have no wish to get to know the nature of the thing from the word. Who has ever thought of lime at the mention of *calx*? What harm can there be in calling comets comets, that is to say long-haired stars, and what point would there be in calling them flaming-stars or steaming-stars? (Shooting-stars likewise.) It is seldom possible to introduce much into names, so that one has in any case to know the thing first. *Parabola, hyperbola, ellipse* are names of a kind of which chemistry can hardly boast, for they express qualities of these lines from which all the others can be derived – though this, to be sure, is to be ascribed more to the pure nature of the science to which these considerations belong than to any especial imaginativeness on the part of the inventors of these names. But of what use is this wisdom: we employ them as we do the names *circle* and *ring*, or *conchoid*, which are not definitions. The dispute is indeed somewhat similar to the purist endeavours of the language-reformers and orthographers. *Too much* is expected of good words and feared from bad ones. It is not only the correctness of an expression that counts but also its familiarity, and the value of a word thus to a certain extent consists in the relative combination of correctness and familiarity whenever the word is used. To lay down rules for the creation of words is, to be sure, always a very good thing, for a time may come when they are needed. It really is a good thing to give things Greek names. If all the names in chemistry were Hebrew or Arabic names, such as *alkali* etc., one would get on better with it the less one understood the names.

6

Nomenclature. Here too a limited monarchy is to be preferred to an aristocracy. If we want to allow validity only to rationally selected expressions there will be an aristocracy, and then which are the most rational and who is to decide the issue? For there are many expressions that might be selected that are all equally good and equally rational. Here too I consider a carved monarch the best monarch; carved saints accomplish more than living ones. Vanity always plays a bigger part in the remodelling of imported names than does utility, for usually they become useful only when we accept them as we did the old ones – when, that is, we cease to think *of the nature of the things* they designate and think only of the things themselves. Hypotheses are opinions, nomenclatures are mandates.

7

Nomenclature. I always believe it is best not to reform at all. It arouses animosity and envy and contempt, and *too much* is written about names that is really of no value whatever. The senseless disappears of itself, and that which is as it were an affront to nature does not grow again.

8

I am extraordinarily susceptible to loud noises, but they lose all their disagreeableness as soon as they are connected with some rational objective.

9

I have frequently been censured for errors I have committed which those who have censured me had not the energy or the wit to commit themselves.

10

In all that I do and do not do, nothing pains me more than the fact that I am obliged to view the world just as the ordinary man does, even though as a scientist I know he views it erroneously.

11

Where foresight was useless I possessed it; but where it could have been of some use I became thoughtless and frivolous: *Kommt Zeit, kommt Rat*, I thought – when the time comes I will know what to do – and did nothing. It is a disposition far more common than we think.

12

Even if my philosophy does not extend to discovering anything new, it does nevertheless possess the courage to regard as questionable what has long been thought true.

13

Nothing makes one old so quickly as the ever-present thought that one is growing older . . .

14

What makes it so difficult to study a profound philosophy is the fact that in everyday life we regard a host of things as being so natural and easy we find it impossible to believe they could ever be any different; and yet we have to be told we must perceive that these supposed trivia are of the greatest weightiness and consequence in order that what is pronounced *difficult* about them shall then be explained. When I say: *this stone is hard* – thus first attribute the concept *stone*, which is composed of several factors, to this *individuo*, then speak of hardness, and then go on to unite this being hard with the stone – this is such a miracle of an operation it is a question whether so much has been expended on the production of whole books. 'But is this not a subtlety? do you need to know it?' – As to the first question: it is not a subtlety, for it is to precisely these simple instances that we are obliged to have recourse in order to get to know the operations of the faculty of reason . . . As regards the other question, however, I reply: *No!* you don't need to know it; but neither do you need to be a philosopher.

15

What is very strange and unusual seldom remains unexplained for long. The inexplicable is usually no longer strange and unusual and perhaps never has been.

16

Reason grasps theory very well; *judicium* decides its application. Very many people are deficient in the latter, and often the greatest scholars and theoreticians are deficient in it most of all.

17

The prerogatives of *beauty* and *happiness* are quite different from one another. For one to enjoy the advantages of beauty *other* people have to believe one is beautiful; there is no necessity at all for this, however, in the case of happiness: that one believes it *oneself* is perfectly sufficient.

18

We should say *it thinks*, just as we say *it lightens*. To say *cogito* is already to say too much as soon as we translate it *I think*. To assume, to postulate the *I* is a practical requirement.

19

What does it mean to *think in the spirit of Kant?* I believe it means to find out what the relationships are that obtain between our being, whatever it may be, and those things we say are *outside us*; that is to say, to determine the relationship of the subjective to the objective. This has, to be sure, always been the goal of all thorough natural philosophers: the question is whether they have ever set about it in so truly philosophical a way as Herr Kant . . .

20

I can never see anything wrong with theorizing: it is an impulse of the soul that can prove useful to us as soon as we have accumulated sufficient experience. Thus all the follies of theorizing we at present commit could be impulses that will find their application only in the future.

21

Man is to be found in reason, God in the passions. I believe Pope has already said something of the sort.

22

Is it not strange that belief can grow stronger than reason? And is the question not which of them has more right to direct our actions, since they both direct them equally strongly when they begin to dominate?

23

The prospect of mankind's progress towards greater perfection seems a dismal one when we consult the analogue of all that lives.

24

Our inability to learn in later years is connected with our unwillingness to take orders in later years, and is so very closely.

25

It is impossible to see any limit to the distance anthropomorphism can extend, the word taken in its largest compass. People revenge themselves on the dead; bones are exhumed and dishonoured; we take pity on inanimate objects – thus someone once commiserated with a clock when it stopped because of the cold. This transference of our feelings to others is to be found everywhere, and in such manifold forms it is not always easy to identify it. Perhaps the entire pronoun *other* originates in this way.

26

Since in dreams we so often take our own objections for those of *another*, e.g. when we are disputing with someone, I am only surprised we do not frequently do so when awake. The condition of wakefulness thus seems to lie chiefly in our making a sharp and conventional distinction between *in us* and *outside us*.

27

The sure conviction that we could if we wanted to is the reason so many good minds are idle.

28

In the weak, lack of strength to defend oneself passes over into complaining. This can be observed in children when they are mistreated by bigger children; but the best always stay obstinately and defiantly silent.

29

To be content with life – or to live merrily, rather – all that is required is that we bestow on all things only a fleeting, superficial glance; the more thoughtful we become the more earnest we grow.

30

Every German village has its Pyramid: the church steeple . . . Why did they build such tall structures? Certainly not solely on account of the bells. Vanity, mixed with religion and perhaps superstition, was what created these Pyramids – in Germany just as much as in Egypt.

31

I once knew a miller's boy who never removed his cap when he met me unless he had a donkey walking beside him. For a long time I could not explain it. At length I discovered that he regarded this company as a humiliation and was pleading for compassion; by removing his cap he seemed to want to evade the slightest comparison between himself and his companion.

32

To this hour I cannot really understand why little children are not just as constantly laughing as they are constantly crying.

33

It is certainly better not to have studied a subject at all than to have studied it superficially. For when unaided healthy common sense seeks to form an opinion of something it does not go so far wrong as semi-erudition does.

34

The greater the man, the more culpable he is if he blabs about the faults of people he knows. If God proclaimed the secrets of men the world could not endure. It would be as though you could see other people's thoughts . . .

35

There are a host of little moral duplicities we practise without believing we are doing any harm; just as, for instance, we smoke tobacco with a similar indifference to our health.

36

Pride, a noble passion, is not blind to its own faults, but *haughtiness* is.

37

If only a tenth part of the religion and morality to be found in books could be found in the hearts of men! But it is almost everywhere the case that soon after it is begotten the greater part of human wisdom is laid to rest in *repositories*. That is why someone once suggested that this word derives, not from the Latin *reponere*, but directly from the French *repos*.*

38

To make a vow is a greater sin than to break one.

39

Before we blame we should first see whether we cannot excuse.

40

Man loves company, even if it is only that of a smouldering candle.

41

He who says he hates every kind of flattery, and says it in earnest, certainly does not yet know every kind of flattery . . .

42

To receive applause for works which do not demand all our powers hinders our advance towards a perfecting of our spirit. It usually means that thereafter we stand still. That is why Rochefoucauld believed that no man had ever yet done all it was in his power to do; I believe this is true for the greater part of mankind. Every human soul has its portion of indolence which makes it tend chiefly to do that which comes easy to it.

43

One of the greatest and at the same time commonest human errors is to believe that, because we do not hear our failings talked about or see them discussed in print, other people do not know of them. I believe, however, that most people are known by others better than they are known to themselves. I know that celebrated writers who were however at bottom shallow-pates (a combination frequently found in Germany) have, all their self-conceit notwithstanding, been regarded as shallow-pates by the best minds I was able to interrogate on the matter.

44

Is it possible to blush in the dark? I am sure we can go pale with fear in the dark, but I don't believe we can blush. For we go pale on account of ourself, but we blush on account of ourself and another . . .

45

I believe that so-called truly devout people are not good because they are devout but devout because they are good. There are certain characters to whom it is natural to reconcile themselves to all the circumstances of domestic and civil life, and to put up with those things which they see as in part useful and in part impossible to improve upon. Thus to ascribe this to religion could well be a *fallacia causae*.

46

I have found throughout my life that, if all else fails, the character of a man can be recognized by nothing so surely as by a jest which he takes badly.

47

He was one of those who want to do everything better than you ask them to. This is a frightful quality in a servant.

48

It is in the gift for employing all the vicissitudes of life to one's own advantage and to that of one's craft that a large part of genius consists.

49

If you want to see what man could do if he wanted to you have only to think of those who have broken out of prison or tried to break out. They have done as much with a single nail as they could have with a battering-ram.

50

Those who never have time do least.

51

The innovations of genius are big and bold, and are often profound, but the power to make them dies early. Sober reason is not so daringly innovative but endures longer. One is rarely an impulsive innovator after the age of sixty, but one can still be a very fine orderly and inventive thinker. One rarely procreates children at that age, but one is all the more skilled at educating those who have already been procreated, and education is procreation of another kind.

52

So-called professional mathematicians have, in their reliance on the relative incapacity of the rest of mankind, acquired for themselves a reputation for profundity very similar to the reputation for sanctity possessed by theologians.

53

The celebrated wit Chamfort used to say: I have three kinds of friends: those who love me, those who pay no attention to me, and those who detest me. Very true!

54

Out of an exaggerated care to avoid a disaster you do precisely that which brings one down upon you, whereas *if you had done nothing* you would certainly have been safe: this is one of the most annoying of situations to be in. For in addition to the unpleasantness of the thing itself you have also the mortification of self-reproach and of having made yourself ludicrous in the eyes of others. I have seen someone smash a valuable vase by trying to move it from where it had been standing quietly for at least six months simply because he was afraid it might one day be accidentally knocked over.

55

First we *have* to believe, and then we believe.

56

If chance had not worked its dextrous hand into our educational system what would have become of our world?

57

It is always dangerous times when men have a lively awareness of their own importance and of what they have the power to do. It is always a good thing for them to slumber a little in regard to their political rights, powers and possibilities, just as horses ought not to employ their strength on every possible occasion.

58

If freedom is natural to man, as they say it is, is it any less natural for him to submit to the protection of another if he is insufficiently strong or active? Since men have thought themselves superior to kings, will there not always be those who think themselves superior to the law? ... Men have thought themselves superior to kings, but not because the kings were tyrants; they have called kings tyrants so that they could think themselves superior to them. And what if there should from now on never be any lack of ambitious men who regard the law as a tyrant?

59

It almost seems as though knowledge of certain truths and their application in life suffers the same fate as the plants: when they have reached a certain height they are cut off so as to begin again from the beginning. The highest degree of political freedom borders directly on despotism. How fine a thing it is that the English constitution should have taken the precaution of combining republican freedom with the monarchy, so as to prevent a complete overturn out of a democracy into pure monarchy or despotism!

60

The saddest thing the French Revolution has brought about is incontestably that every reasonable demand crying out to God and law for redress will be seen as the germ of rebellion.

61

The issue is not whether the sun never sets on a monarch's domains, as Spain formerly boasted, but what it gets to see in these domains during the course of its progress.

62

To establish liberty and equality as many people now think of them would mean producing an eleventh commandment through which the other ten would be abolished.

63

What the great have now to reflect on is that they certainly cannot easily oppress their subjects more sternly than they were oppressed in France, and yet the oppressed of France have cut their king's head off.

64

It is a great question whether more has been accomplished in the world through what has been well thought or through what has been merely well said. To think something through to the bottom and at the same time to express it really well is not easy; in any event, at the moment the beauty of expression is felt the thought being expressed has not yet been fully recognized. The political writings published nowadays in France are censured as shallow rigmarole. I think this censure is itself somewhat shallow and reveals a lack of understanding of human nature. For these books are written, not for the human race in general or for abstract reason, but for concrete people of a certain party; and they certainly achieve *their goal* more surely than do those calculated for that abstract man who has never yet existed and never will exist.

65

There is, I believe, no question but that, all inequality of rank notwithstanding, all men can be *equally happy*; all we have to do is try to make everyone as happy as possible.

66

I believe that some of the greatest minds that have ever lived had not read half as much and did not know nearly as much as many of our mediocre scholars. And many of our very mediocre scholars would have been greater men if they had not read so much.

67

What lies in the way of many a writer's fame and immortality more effectively than the envy and malice of all the critical journals and magazines put together is the unfortunate circumstance that they are obliged to have their works printed on a material that can also be used as grocers' paper-bags.

68

What I do not like about the way history is treated is that intention is seen in every action and every event attributed to intention. This, however, is truly quite false. The greatest events occur without intention playing any part in them; chance makes good mistakes and undoes the most carefully planned undertaking. The world's greatest events are not produced, they happen.

69

There can hardly be stranger wares in the world than *books*: printed by people who do not understand them; sold by people who do not understand them; bound, reviewed and read by people who do not understand them; and now even written by people who do not understand them.

70

Many priests of Minerva also possess, in addition to those they share with the goddess herself, certain similarities to her celebrated bird: though they are able to catch mice in the dark, in daylight they cannot see the church steeple before they have shattered their heads against it.

71

Would it not be much better for the human race if we no longer had any history at all, or at least no political history? Men would act more in accord with the powers they possess on each particular occasion; whereas now, for every one who is improved by the example of the past a thousand are made worse.

72

There is no greater impediment to progress in the sciences than the desire to see it take place too quickly. This is very characteristic of brisk and lively people, which is why they seldom achieve very much: for they are cast down and give up as soon as they perceive they are not advancing. Yet they would have advanced if they had used less energy and taken more time.

73

A sad reflection on the history of the ancient world is presented to us by that of modern France. How much has been written about France! But, this notwithstanding, who would now think himself wise enough to write about it anything that came anywhere near the truth? Less was written in the ancient world, to be sure, and consequently less has been read, but certainly just as much happened; what is the worst, indeed, is that here we are thus obliged to rely more on tales and tradition.

74

The only fault one can impute to genuinely fine writings is that they are usually the cause of very many bad or mediocre ones.

75

Mathematics is a glorious science indeed, but mathematicians are often not worth a light. In mathematics things stand almost as they do in theology. Just as those engaged in the latter, especially when they occupy official positions, lay claim to a special reputation for sanctity and a closer relationship with God, although very many of them are in fact real good-for-nothings, so the so-called mathematicians very often demand that they be regarded as profound thinkers, although there are likewise among them the biggest trash-heads to be found anywhere, useless for any employment that demands thinking unless it can be carried out through that easy linking together of symbols that is the work of routine rather than of thought.

76

It would have to be a quite fearfully dreadful translation that could spoil a good book for a man of intelligence who reads it as a whole without lingering over individual expressions or sentences. A book which does not possess this quality and which even the worst translator can hardly spoil for a man of intelligence is certainly not written for posterity.

77

Some time ago it was the fashion, and perhaps it is so still, to append to the title of a novel the words: *a true story*. Well, that is a little innocent deception; but that the words *a novel* are omitted from many recent history books is not so innocent a deception.

78

Perhaps many a bad book now the object of contempt will one day perform for a good one precisely the service the wretched plays that were contemporary with Shakespeare's have performed for them. Thus even to the bad writer there comes the consolation that posterity will one day recognize his merits.

79

Just as people must have knives and pistols taken away from them when they are drunk, so under the same circumstances they ought to have their purses taken away from them, for fear they do too much good.

80

It would, to be sure, be a good thing if there were no suicides. But let us not judge too hastily. How in the world could we, e.g. in tragedies, get rid of characters no longer of any use? To have them murdered by others is a dangerous practice. All is ordered for the best.

81

There are so many geniuses about nowadays we ought to be right glad when Heaven for once bestows upon us a child who isn't one.

82

Nowadays we everywhere seek to propagate wisdom: who knows whether in a couple of centuries there may not exist universities for restoring the old ignorance?

83

Would it not be a good thing if in say the year 1800 we were to assume that theology is concluded and forbid theologians to make any further discoveries?

84

To call a proposition into question all that is needed is very often merely to fail to understand it. Certain gentlemen have been all too ready to reverse this maxim, and to assert that we fail to understand their propositions if we call them into question.

85

The Socratic method *intensified* – I mean *torture*.

86

A girl scarcely twelve *fashions* old.

87

Where the common people take pleasure in puns, and often make them themselves, you may always count upon it that the nation stands on a very high rung of culture. The peasants of Calenberg make no puns.

88

To sit and worry about what we *might have done* is the worst thing we *can do*.

89

What is said of the benefits and disadvantages of the *Enlightenment* can be well represented in a fable of fire. It is the soul of inorganic nature, its use in moderation makes life pleasant for us, it warms our winters and illuminates our nights. But that must be done with torches and candles: to illuminate the streets by setting fire to houses is a very ill form of illumination. Nor must children be allowed to play with it.

90

If they were to report the facts about patients who have *not* been helped by certain health spas and watering-places, and report them with the same conscientiousness as they report the opposite, no one would any longer visit them – at least, no invalid would.

91

Whenever someone makes badly what we expected to be well made, we say: *I could do as well as that myself.* There are few expressions that betray so much modesty.

92

I have had all last year's newspapers bound up together, and the effect of reading them is indescribable: 50 parts false hopes, 47 parts false prophecies and three parts truth. This reading has lowered my opinion of this year's papers very greatly, for I reflect: what the latter are the former were also.

93
If fish are dumb, fishwives make up for it.

94
We live in a world in which one fool can make many fools but one wise man only a few wise ones.

95
The German Pantheon. I have stood before Newton's monument in Westminster Abbey; I have seen Shakespeare's memorial together with those of great heroes; only I have to confess, perhaps to my shame, that the impression I have received was very mixed and peculiar. I found it impossible to convince myself that Newton and Shakespeare were honoured by them: it seemed to me, on the contrary, that these memorials stood there to honour the others and to bestow honour on the place where they stood. I found it impossible to rid myself of this feeling. – What good would it be to instal Luther in a German Pantheon? Would it bestow honour on Luther? Certainly not: it would bestow honour on the Pantheon. If such an institution is to be of any use at all men must be installed there whose deeds were great without glory, who acquired merit simply through acts for their country and their fellow men – no writers as such. A writer who needs a statue to immortalize him is not worthy of one.

96
In England it has been suggested that thieves should be castrated. It is not a bad suggestion: the punishment is very severe, it renders those who suffer it contemptible and yet still capable of employment; and if stealing is hereditary it is no longer passed on. Courage is abated, too, and since the sexual drive so often leads to thieving this instigation is also suppressed. The observation that women would be all the more eager to restrain their men from stealing is merely jocular: for as things are they stand to lose them altogether.

97

Since the invention of writing *requests* have lost much of their force, while *commands* have grown more forceful. That is an ill balance-account. Written requests are easier to reject and written commands easier to give than oral ones. Both require a heart that is often lacking when the mouth has to speak.

98

It is so very modern to place a funeral urn on top of a grave while the body rots in a box underneath. And this funeral urn is in turn a mere symbol of a funeral urn: it is merely the tombstone of a funeral urn.

99

I have read Heydenreich's *Letters on Atheism*, and I have to confess that, contrary to his intention, the letters of the atheist seem to me to be very much more profound than those of the believers. I am not so wholly unacquainted with the exertion of my reason, nor do I lack good will, but I am none the less unable to be convinced of the truth of certain of the believers' assertions. Too much reliance is placed on the dissemination of a moral consciousness, and I might almost say that behind this proposition there lies concealed the intention of making us believe by asserting that we must be morally sick if we fail to understand what is being said. If the inventors of these well-meant propositions possessed a recognized infallibility we could *accustom* ourselves to regarding their propositions as true, and they for their part could declare: thy belief hath made thee whole. – But what for mankind is the point of a demonstration of the existence of God and immortality which hardly one in a thousand is capable of understanding or of really *feeling* the truth of? If belief in God and immortality is to be of any real use in a world such as this it must become more easily available, or it is as good as none at all.

100

Yesterday it rained all day and today the sun shone all day. How many events of my life would have taken a different direction if it had rained today and the sun had shone yesterday? The winter of 1794–95 was fearfully severe, that of 1795–96 very mild. What world events would have taken a different direction if this order had been reversed?

Certainly the French would not have conquered Holland. Reflections of this sort can take us very far.

101

I would give something to know for precisely whom the deeds were really done of which it is publicly stated they were done *for the Fatherland*.

102

It is true I cannot say whether things are going to change for the better, but what I do say is that things will never be right unless they do change.

103

There are countries where it is not uncommon for officers who have served well in a war to be reduced in rank when peace arrives. Would it not be a good thing if in certain departments of government the officials, or some of them, were reduced in rank whenever war breaks out? It would be quite enough, indeed, if they were merely reduced to half-pay.

104

We ought not to lie down to sleep without being able to say we have learned something that day. By this I do not mean, for instance, a word we didn't know before; such a thing is nothing; but if anyone wants to do it I have nothing against it, not just before blowing out the light in any event. No, what I mean by learning is the advancement of our scientific or otherwise useful knowledge; the rectification of an error in which we have long been involved; the acquisition of certainty in many things about which we were for long uncertain and of a clear conception of that which was unclear to us; a knowledge of important truths, etc. What makes this endeavour useful is that we cannot take care of the matter quickly just before blowing out the light: our activities throughout the whole day have to be directed towards it. Even the will to fulfil such resolutions is important: I mean here the constant endeavour to satisfy the requirement.

105

Doubt everything at least once, even the proposition that two times two equals four.

1796–1799

1

The great are often reproached with having failed to do much good they could have done. They might reply: just think of the evil we could have done and did *not* do.

2

Great conquerors are always gazed at with admiration and the history of the world is divided up according to their careers. This is a sad fact, but it lies in human nature . . . At a cattle-market everyone always looks at the biggest and fattest oxen.

3

That sermons are preached in churches doesn't mean the churches don't need lightning-conductors.

4

He stomped slowly and proudly ahead like a hexameter, and his wife came tripping along after him like a pentameter.

5

The Greeks did not ruin the best years of their youth by learning *dead languages*; instead they learned the languages they had need of, and did so through the things described and not, as we do in countless instances, the things described through the words. Plutarch was already getting on when he started to learn Latin.

6

The windows of the Enlightenment are subject to a heavy window-tax in Germany.

7

Someone was asked to give a definition of God: God, he said, is a sphere whose centre is everywhere and whose surface is nowhere.

8

I think it would be worthwhile for once to represent the calumnies of the coffee-table as a game of cards, with each playing against the other. Pope's *Rape of the Lock* could serve as a model. One lady trumping another's scandal.

9

I have long been convinced that in families which consist, for example, of a husband and wife, four to eight children, a chambermaid, a couple of maid-servants, a couple of footmen, a coachman, etc., and likewise in smaller families, especially when a couple of elderly aunts are at any rate tolerated in it as well, affairs are conducted precisely as, *mutatis mutandis*, they are in the greatest states: here too there are agreements, peace treaties, wars, changes of ministry, *lettres de cachet*, Reformations, revolutions, etc. . . .

10

Defence of the monastic life is usually founded on a wholly erroneous concept of virtue . . .

11

Whether the amount of distress in Germany has increased I do not know, but the number of exclamation marks certainly has. Where we formerly had merely! we now have!!!

12

A somewhat pert philosopher – Hamlet, Prince of Denmark, I think – said there were more things in Heaven and earth than could be found in our compendia. If the simple fellow, who as is well known was not in his right mind, was with this phrase jeering at our compendia of physics, we may cheerfully reply to him: very good, but on the other hand there are more things in our compendia than can be found in either Heaven or earth.

13

Whisper, immortal muse, of the insanity of the great.

14

My inquiries into physics could perhaps be given the title: *legacies*. For people do also bequeath trifles, after all.

15

As he walked past the churchyard he said: Those in there can now be sure they aren't going to be hanged, which is more than we can.

16

A few days ago I again read of a clergyman in, if I am not mistaken, Liége, who died aged 125 and was supposed to have been asked by his bishop what he had done to become so old. 'I have,' he said, 'abstained from wine, women and wrath.' The great question here, it seems to me, is: did the man become so old because he abstained from these poisons or because he possessed a temperament that made it possible for him to abstain from them? I believe it impossible not to opt for the latter . . . He who does not have the temperament would certainly *not* prolong his life by abstaining from the opposite sex. It is the same with the saying that true Christians are always honest people. There were honest people long before there were Christians and there are, God be praised, still honest people where there are no Christians. It could therefore easily be possible that people are Christians because true Christianity corresponds to what they would have been even if Christianity did not exist. Socrates would certainly have been a very good Christian.

17

We now possess four principles of morality:
1 *a philosophical*: do good for its own sake, out of respect for the law;
2 *a religious*: do good because it is God's will, out of love of God;
3 *a human*: do good because it will promote your *happiness*, out of self-love;
4 *a political*: do good because it will promote the welfare of the society of which you are a part, out of love of society having regard to yourself. (All this is from the *Reichs-Anzeiger*, No. 133. 1797 (Düvel).) But is this not all one single principle, only viewed from different sides? . . .

18

He who desires to raise his children to become whores and rogues . . . must above all take care to acquaint them with the rudiments before the children discover they are vices.

19

It is possible that many facets of the Kantian philosophy may never be *completely* understood by anyone, and that each will believe the other understands it better than he and will consequently be satisfied with a vague insight into it or even sometimes believe it is his own incapacity that is preventing him from seeing it as clearly as others do.

20

One usually begins one's last will and testament by commending one's soul to God. I shall forbear to do this, because I believe that such recommendations are of little avail: if they have not been preceded by a whole recommendable life, such recommendations are gallows-conversions – as easy as they are null and void.

21

At times when people thought I was very busy I have often been giving myself up to all kinds of dreams and fantasies for hours on end. I have felt how disadvantageous this is as regards waste of time, yet without this *fantasy cure*, which I usually had recourse to at the time people take the waters, I should not have reached the age I have, which is 53 years 1 ½ months.

22

He didn't *want* to corrupt, but he *did* corrupt. It is very sad that the endeavour to diminish the evil with which man is plagued only serves to augment it. As a rule it seems we are better acquainted with the force than we are with the material to which it is applied.

23

If this is philosophy it is at any rate a philosophy that is not in its right mind.

24

Everything we as men are *compelled* to recognize as real really is real for men. For as soon as it is no longer permitted to conclude that what natural constraint tells us is actual is in fact actual any firm principle ceases to be conceivable. One thing is then as uncertain as another. He to whom the proof of the existence of a supreme being from nature (the cosmological proof) is compelling, let him accept it; likewise he who finds the theoretical or the moral proof convincing. Even those who have racked their brains to discover new proofs have perhaps been induced to do so by a compulsion they could not quite explain to themselves. Instead of giving us their new proofs they should have explained to us the motivation that constrained them to search for them, provided it was not merely fear of consistories or governments.

25

Alas, what would *we* do, said the girl, if God did not exist?

26

The 'second sight' possessed by the Highlanders in Scotland is actually a foreknowledge of future events. I believe they possess this gift because they don't wear trousers. That is also why in all countries women are more prone to utter prophecies.

27

Is it not strange that you can attain to the highest position of honour in the world (king) without passing an examination demanded of any town physician?

28

Voltaire says somewhere very truly: *Si Dieu n'existait, il falloit l'inventer.*

29

Kant says somewhere: Reason is rather polemical than dogmatic.

30

On 22 October 97 Herr Thibaut, a man of excellent understanding, said to me that certain concepts of ordinary arithmetic gave him more difficulty than many concepts of the higher calculus usually considered difficult.

31

The only way of venerating God is to do our duty and to act in accordance with the laws reason has given us. *There is a God* can, in my view, mean nothing other than: with all my freedom of will, I feel myself compelled to do *right* . . . A God who intervenes objectively when I do wrong does not exist: that is the task of the judge who administers the law, or it is our own task. That is why I likewise do not believe there exist any mockers of religion, though there certainly are mockers of theology . . .

32

It is a question whether reason alone without the heart would ever have conceived of a God. After the heart (fear) had apprehended him reason sought him too, in the way Bürger sought after ghosts.*

33

I now do really believe that the question whether objects outside of us possess objective reality fails to make rational sense. We are *compelled* by our nature to say of certain objects of our perception that they are located outside of us, we cannot do otherwise . . . The question is almost as foolish as the question whether the colour blue is really *blue*. We cannot possibly transcend the question . . .

34

Of all the inventions of man I doubt whether any was more easily accomplished than that of a Heaven.

35

Her physical charms were at just that curious moment when their power of attraction began to change into their power of repulsion.

36

Are we too not a cosmic system, and one we know better, or at least ought to know better, than we do the heavenly firmament?

37

What makes true friendship, and even more the happy bond of marriage, so delightful is the extension of one's ego it involves, and an extension indeed over a field which no art in the world can create within an individual person. Two souls which unite together none the less do not unite so completely as to obliterate that mutually advantageous difference between them that makes *communication* so pleasant. He who bewails his sorrows to himself certainly does so in vain, he who bewails them to his wife bewails them to a self that can aid him and does so already in the act of sympathy. He who likes to hear himself praised likewise finds in her a public before whom he can boast without making himself ludicrous.

38

Has the soul not got itself into a strange situation when it reads an investigation of itself – that is to say, seeks in books for what it itself might be? It is somewhat similar to a dog that has had a bone tied to its tail – said Lion, with truth but somewhat ignobly.

39

When he philosophizes he usually throws a pleasant moonlight over the objects of his philosophizing which is pleasing as a whole but fails to display clearly one single object.

40

The French Revolution: experimental politics.

41

Even the gentlest, most modest and best of girls are always better, gentler and more modest if their mirrors have told them they are looking more beautiful than ever.

42

It is a good thing that lack of thought does not produce the same effect as lack of air, or many a head that ventures to read works it does not understand would collapse in on itself.

43

It is certain, indeed, that we can judge of a thing very well and wisely, and yet as soon as we are required to give our reasons we are able to give only such reasons as any novice in the art of thrust and parry can refute . . .

44

Actual aristocracy cannot be abolished by any law: all the law can do is decree how it is to be imparted and who is to acquire it.

45

This was the handle by which you had to grip him if you wanted to pour him out: if you gripped him anywhere else you burned your fingers.

46

I am afraid that the excessively careful education we provide is cultivating dwarf fruit.

47

When negro servants in the West Indies mix a punch they first ask: for drunk or for dry? We might ask something of the sort before political disputes: shall we dispute with feeling or with reason, for drunk or for dry?

48

His conscience was elevated to an earldom.

49

What most clearly characterizes true freedom and its true employment is its misemployment.

50

Reason now gazes above the realm of the dark but warm feelings as the Alpine peaks do above the clouds. They behold the sun more clearly and distinctly, but they are cold and unfruitful . . .

51

Van Kempelen's machine says the words Papa and Roma best: that's curious, a Jesuit would say.

52

Motto: to desire to discover the truth is meritorious, even if we go astray on the way.

53

Where everybody wants to come as early as possible it must necessarily follow that by far the greater number come too late.

54

Germany has behaved in a truly Christian fashion towards unchristian France. When the latter had smitten it on one cheek it turned the other.

55

The lines of humanity and urbanity do not coincide.

56

The reason the prefaces to many books are often so strangely written is that they have been written while their authors were still in the grip of scholarly childbed-fever.

57

We talk a lot about Enlightenment and desire more light. But, my God, what is the use of light if people either have no eyes or intentionally shut those they have?

58

I have again started eating everything forbidden me and, praise be to God, I feel just as bad as I did before (I mean no worse).

59

When we are young we scarcely know we are alive. We acquire the feeling of health only through sickness. That the earth draws us towards it becomes apparent when we jump into the air through the blow we receive on falling. When age sets in the state of being sick becomes a species of health and we no longer notice we are sick. If recollection of the past did not stay with us we would notice little of the change. I therefore also believe that animals grow old only from our point of view of them. A squirrel which on the day of its death leads the life of an oyster is no more unhappy than the oyster. Man, however, who lives in three places – in the past, in the present and in the future – can be unhappy if one of these three is worthless. Religion has even added a fourth – eternity.

60

The celebrated painter Gainsborough got as much pleasure from seeing violins as from hearing them.

61

If need is the mother of industriousness or of invention, it is a question who the father is, or the grandmother, or who the mother of need is.

62

It is possible to stroke someone's cheek in such a way that a third party feels as if he has had his ears boxed.

63

How much in the world depends on presentation is already evident from the fact that coffee drunk out of a wineglass is a very unpleasant drink, or from the sight of meat being cut at table with a pair of scissors . . .

64

Woe to the genius in countries where there are no earthquakes.

65

If *need* is the mother of invention, then the war that begot the need is no doubt the grandfather of invention . . .

66

Diminution of one's needs is something that certainly ought to be inculcated in youth. 'The fewer needs one has the happier one is' is an old but much-neglected truth.

67

If we did not remember our youth we should not be aware of old age: the malady of age consists solely in our no longer being able to do what we could do formerly. For the old man is certainly as perfect a creature in his own way as is the young.

68

When Moritz bewailed the fact that he had to die so young, Hofrat Herz of Berlin told him he should imagine he was born in 1712. A foolish idea.

69

It is good when young people are in certain years attacked by the poetic infection, only one must, for Heaven's sake, not neglect to inoculate them against it.

70

He was always smoothing and polishing himself, and in the end he became blunt before he was sharp.

71

I would have given a part of my life to know what the average height of the barometer was in Paradise.

72

In many matters habit is an evil thing. It makes us take injustice for justice and error for truth.

73

There are people with so little courage to assert anything that they dare not say there is a cold wind blowing, however much they may feel it, unless they have first heard that other people have said it.

74

A real arrest-warrant face.

75

The inhabitants of the *Friendly* Islands are continually at war and even eat one another. Even *here* civility towards guests is completely compatible with domestic abominableness.

76

It is almost impossible to write anything good without imagining someone, or a certain group of people, whom one is addressing. In 999 cases out of a thousand it at any rate greatly facilitates the execution.

77

The question is still whether in the last resort the spirit of contradiction is not on the whole of greater utility than unity and agreement.

78

I have noticed a *hundred times*, and do not doubt that many of my readers must have noticed *a hundred-and-one or a hundred-and-two times*, that books with an arresting, imaginative title are seldom worth much. It is to be presumed they were invented *before* the book itself, frequently perhaps by someone else.

79

If they were to stand fast we would regard even shooting-stars as stars.

80

Nothing cheers me up so much as when I have succeeded in understanding something difficult, and yet I try so little to learn to understand difficult things. I ought to try to more often.

81

With most people disbelief in a thing is founded on a blind belief in some other thing.

82

At his birth everyone receives a ticket in the great lottery of discovery in which the biggest prize had certainly not yet been drawn by the end of the year 1798.

83

In England a man was charged with bigamy and his lawyer got him off by proving that his client had three wives.

84

Not to be forgotten: that I once wrote down the question What are the northern lights? and left it in Graupner's garret addressed to an angel, and next morning crept quietly back to collect the note. Oh if only there had been some little rascal to reply to that note!*

85

Is it not strange that men are so keen to *fight* for religion and so unkeen to *live* according to its precepts?

86

If physics is to progress it is absolutely necessary that there should be more minds which comprehend the whole. This is surely the rarest class of mind. We want to know the nature of the palace in which we dwell. So a man comes along with a splinter he has taken from the doorstep and shows us he has made a toothpick out of it and that it burns when held against a candle. A second man knocks a piece off a roof-tile and shows that it contains iron, flint and clay. A third attacks a door-knob, a fourth attacks the panelling and concludes that the whole building is constructed of *toothpick material* . . .

87

What Kant really says is: we presuppose that things-in-themselves lie behind all phenomena, but we do not know whether reality can be ascribed to this presupposition, whether it in fact corresponds to that which is presupposed.

88

There exists no bridge that leads beyond our thoughts to the objects of them.

89

With just the same degree of certainty with which we are convinced that something occurs *within us* we are also convinced that something occurs *outside us*. We understand the words *inside* and *outside* very well. There can be no one in the world, or who will ever be born, who is not sensible of this *distinction*; and for philosophy that suffices. It should not seek to transcend it; to do so would be to toil in vain and to waste one's time. For whatever may be the nature of things, it seems to have been arranged and settled that we can simply know nothing of them except that which lies in our ideas of them: and from this point of view, which I believe to be correct, the question whether things are really present outside of us, and are present in the form in which we see them, is truly totally without meaning. Is it not strange that man absolutely demands to have something twice when once would have been enough, and necessarily has to be enough because there exists no bridge between our ideas and the causes of them? We cannot think that anything can exist without a cause, but where then does this necessity lie? The answer again is *within us*, in as much as it is completely impossible for us to go out of ourselves. It truly matters little to me whether or not one wishes to call this idealism. Names are of no account. It is at any rate an idealism that recognizes through idealism that there are things outside of it and that everything has its causes: what more do you want? For there is no other reality for men, at least not for the philosophical. In ordinary life we are rightly satisfied with a less exalted situation. But I believe with full conviction: one must either completely abstain from philosophizing about these matters or philosophize *thus*. In the light of all this it is easy to see how right Herr Kant is to regard space and time as mere forms of perception. Nothing else is possible.

90

I do not believe that any great *discovery* has ever been made in the natural sciences through calculation. Nor is this its function. But as soon as chance or practical insight has discovered something, mathematics provides for it the best environment; given that the matter is thus or thus as a whole, mathematics demonstrates the form and disposition most appropriate to it. – Nothing more.

91

Is reason, or perhaps better the understanding, really better situated when it hits upon final causes than when it hits upon a dictate of the heart? For it is still a great question whether what connects us most firmly with the world that surrounds us is reason or the heart.

92

Man has nowadays so far surpassed himself that he even has a science in which all the new inventions are inventions of new errors and all the new discoveries the discoveries of old errors.

93

It is incontestably a blunder on the part of the atomists to *postulate* matter without reflecting that to postulate this as being endowed with thrust, energy and motion is to postulate almost *everything*. For how an atom of a certain configuration comes into existence is no more comprehensible to me than how a sun comes into existence. It is a pity the finest minds so much like to venture into the unfathomable and are happy to hear the crowd express astonishment at their daring, and prefer to be called rash and foolhardy than quiet cultivators of a ground all the world allows to be firm and solid.

94

May not much of what Herr *Kant* teaches, especially in regard to the moral law, not be a consequence of old age, in which passion and inclination have lost their strength and reason alone remains? – If the human race died in possession of all its powers, at 40 say, what consequences would this have for the world? The combination of repose and wisdom in old age produces many strange things. Will there ever be a state in which everyone is slaughtered at 45?

95

Attraction and *repulsion* – we speak of them as of *different* things, and linguistic usage does indeed encourage us to do so. But by ascribing to bodies a force of attraction and denying to them a force of repulsion we are dealing in a *one-sidedness* of which reason cannot approve. We live, to be sure, in the *region* of attraction, in the place where it prevails; our bodies could not exist without it; we are fixed in it, as are our planets and our sun; but without being Jacob Böhm I can imagine a being existing in the region of repulsion that would fill all the heavens.

96

Has it been so very firmly established that our reason can have no knowledge whatever of the supernatural? Is it not possible that man is able to weave his ideas of God just as *purposefully* as the spider does its web for the purpose of catching flies? Or, in other words: can there not exist beings who would admire us on account of our ideas of God and immortality in just the way we admire the spider and the silkworm?

97

Is our conception of God anything more than personified incomprehensibility?

98

I believe that man is in the last resort so free a being that his right *to be* what he believes himself to be cannot be contested.

99

To want to reduce everything in man to simple principles means, it seems to me, in the last resort to presuppose that such a principle *must* exist, and how can this be proved?

B4 J. J. Winckelmann (1717–68), art historian, Friedrich von Hagedorn (1708–54), poet and critic, and G. E. Lessing (1729–81), dramatist and critic, were influential in the formation of German artistic taste during the latter half of the eighteenth century.

B15 C. F. Gellert (1715–69), poet and fabulist, was a great favourite of the middle-class reader (*Fabeln und Erzählungen*, 1746 and 1748), hence the reference to a wigmaker's wish to write like him.

B18 Leeuwenhoek (1632–1723), very famous in his day and still remembered in Lichtenberg's, discovered the existence of infusoria and blood corpuscles; the relevance of his name here is, of course, that these are very small things.

B58 The Herrnhuters were members of a Protestant sect named after Herrnhut, the estate in Oberlausitz where its founder, Count von Zinzendorf (1700–1760), established its headquarters.

C32 The Jacobi here admonished is probably J. G. Jacobi, who was from 1768 prebendary (*Kanonikus*) at Halberstadt and whom Lichtenberg elsewhere compares with Sterne's Yorick.

C43 'Wren' is in German *Zaunkönig* = king of the hedgerow.

D29 Boehme (1575–1624), the theosophist, enjoyed great popularity among the mystically-minded (*Aurora*, 1612, *Mysterium Magnum*, 1623); his vocabulary was notoriously difficult (to Lichtenberg, it seems, impossible) to understand.

D45 Meister taught Lichtenberg applied mathematics at Göttingen.

D65 Sanssouci is Frederick the Great's palace at Potsdam (constructed 1745–7).

E9 Lully is Ramón Lul, the Franciscan mystic who devised a fanciful system of logic (his *Ars Magna*) through which conclusions were derived from a few *a priori* concepts.

E15 Wilkes is John Wilkes (1727–97), the English political agitator.

E41 F. G. Klopstock (1724–1803) was the foremost German poet of the age before that of Goethe; his principal work, the epic poem *Der Messias* (1748–73), won him the title of the German Milton. J. K. Lavater (1741–1801), a Zürich clergyman, attempted in his *Physionomische Fragmente* (1775–8) to found a science of physiognomy' through which character and disposition could be inferred from the face.

E78 Terzi was a tightrope-walker Lichtenberg had seen at Sadler's Wells theatre.

E80 *Götz von Berlichingen* (1773) is Goethe's earliest literary and theatrical success; a *Landes-Vater* is a species of German student song. The point of the aphorism is to assert the Gothic barbarity of *Götz*.

E87 Because in German one speaks of the ear of a needle, in English of the eye.

F114 Jena, where Schiller lived, and Weimar, the home of Goethe, were the twin capitals of eighteenth-century German culture.

F163 'Lion' is one of the names Lichtenberg adopted when he wrote about himself in the third person, i.e. objectively.

G19 'Bedlam' is a contraction of Bethlehem; here it means the hospital of St Mary of Bethlehem, in London, which was used as a home for lunatics.

J35 J. C. Dieterich was Lichtenberg's landlord in Göttingen and for many years also his publisher.

J66 Benjamin Franklin (1706–90), the American statesman, invented the lightning-conductor.

J154 K. is Abraham Kästner (1719–1800), under whom Lichtenberg studied and whose younger colleague he became. Kästner spoke the oration at Lichtenberg's funeral. He was a scholar of learning and ability, but his splenetic and acrimonious disposition earned him the detestation of many who, like Lichtenberg, would otherwise have admired him.

J172 The *Messiade* is Klopstock's *Der Messias*. The reader may recall Johnson's having given a similar demonstration of practical criticism.

J233 D. is Dieterich (also in J240).

K37 *Repositorien* (repositories) in German also means bookshelves.

L32 Bürger is G. A. Bürger (1747–94), the author of the very popular ballad *Lenore* (1773) and other spectral poems.

L84 'Graupner's garret' is the top floor of the boarding-school at Darmstadt which Lichtenberg attended from 1752 to 1761. He afterwards described his years at this school as the happiest of his life.

FURTHER READING

The most detailed discussion of Lichtenberg's thought in English is J. P. Stern's *Lichtenberg: a Doctrine of Scattered Occasions* (Indiana University Press, 1959, and Thames & Hudson, London, 1963). A short biography in English is provided by Carl Brinitzer's *Die Geschichte eines gescheiten Mannes*, translated by Bernard Smith as *A Reasonable Rebel: Georg Christoph Lichtenberg* (Allen & Unwin, London, 1960). *Lichtenberg's Visits to England* (Clarendon Press, Oxford, 1938) is a translation of a selection from his letters from England, and Innes and Gustav Herdan have translated *Lichtenberg's Commentaries on Hogarth's Engravings* (The Cresset Press, London, 1966).

FOR THE BEST IN PAPERBACKS, LOOK FOR THE

In every corner of the world, on every subject under the sun, Penguin represents quality and variety – the very best in publishing today.

For complete information about books available from Penguin – including Pelicans, Puffins, Peregrines and Penguin Classics – and how to order them, write to us at the appropriate address below. Please note that for copyright reasons the selection of books varies from country to country.

In the United Kingdom: Please write to *Dept E.P., Penguin Books Ltd, Harmondsworth, Middlesex, UB7 0DA*

If you have any difficulty in obtaining a title, please send your order with the correct money, plus ten per cent for postage and packaging, to *PO Box No 11, West Drayton, Middlesex*

In the United States: Please write to *Dept BA, Penguin, 299 Murray Hill Parkway, East Rutherford, New Jersey 07073*

In Canada: Please write to *Penguin Books Canada Ltd, 2801 John Street, Markham, Ontario L3R 1B4*

In Australia: Please write to the *Marketing Department, Penguin Books Australia Ltd, P.O. Box 257, Ringwood, Victoria 3134*

In New Zealand: Please write to the *Marketing Department, Penguin Books (NZ) Ltd, Private Bag, Takapuna, Auckland 9*

In India: Please write to *Penguin Overseas Ltd, 706 Eros Apartments, 56 Nehru Place, New Delhi, 110019*

In Holland: Please write to *Penguin Books Nederland B.V., Postbus 195, NL–1380AD Weesp, Netherlands*

In Germany: Please write to *Penguin Books Ltd, Friedrichstrasse 10–12, D–6000 Frankfurt Main 1, Federal Republic of Germany*

In Spain: Please write to *Longman Penguin España, Calle San Nicolas 15, E–28013 Madrid, Spain*

In France: Please write to *Penguin Books Ltd, 39 Rue de Montmorency, F-75003, Paris, France*

In Japan: Please write to *Longman Penguin Japan Co Ltd, Yamaguchi Building, 2–12–9 Kanda Jimbocho, Chiyoda-Ku, Tokyo 101, Japan*

FOR THE BEST IN PAPERBACKS, LOOK FOR THE 🐧

PENGUIN CLASSICS

Pedro de Alarcón	**The Three-Cornered Hat and Other Stories**
Leopoldo Alas	**La Regenta**
Ludovico Ariosto	**Orlando Furioso**
Giovanni Boccaccio	**The Decameron**
Baldassar Castiglione	**The Book of the Courtier**
Benvenuto Cellini	**Autobiography**
Miguel de Cervantes	**Don Quixote**
	Exemplary Stories
Dante	**The Divine Comedy** (in 3 volumes)
	La Vita Nuova
Bernal Diaz	**The Conquest of New Spain**
Carlo Goldoni	**Four Comedies (The Venetian Twins/The Artful Widow/Mirandolina/The Superior Residence)**
Niccolò Machiavelli	**The Discourses**
	The Prince
Alessandro Manzoni	**The Betrothed**
Benito Pérez Galdós	**Fortunata and Jacinta**
Giorgio Vasari	**Lives of the Artists** (in 2 volumes)

and

Five Italian Renaissance Comedies (Machiavelli/**The Mandragola**;
    Ariosto/**Lena**; Aretino/**The Stablemaster**;
    Gl'Intronati/**The Deceived**; Guarini/**The Faithful Shepherd**)
The Jewish Poets of Spain
The Poem of the Cid
Two Spanish Picaresque Novels (Anon/**Lazarillo de Tormes**;
    de Quevedo/**The Swindler**)

FOR THE BEST IN PAPERBACKS, LOOK FOR THE 🐧

PENGUIN CLASSICS

Carl von Clausewitz	**On War**
Friedrich Engels	**The Origins of the Family, Private Property and the State**
Wolfram von Eschenbach	**Parzival**
	Willehalm
Goethe	**Elective Affinities**
	Faust
	Italian Journey 1786–88
	The Sorrows of Young Werther
Jacob and Wilhelm Grimm	**Selected Tales**
E. T. A. Hoffmann	**Tales of Hoffmann**
Henrik Ibsen	**The Doll's House/The League of Youth/The Lady from the Sea**
	Ghosts/A Public Enemy/When We Dead Wake
	Hedda Gabler/The Pillars of the Community/The Wild Duck
	The Master Builder/Rosmersholm/Little Eyolf/ John Gabriel Borkman
	Peer Gynt
Søren Kierkegaard	**Fear and Trembling**
	The Sickness Unto Death
Friedrich Nietzsche	**Beyond Good and Evil**
	Ecce Homo
	A Nietzsche Reader
	Thus Spoke Zarathustra
	Twilight of the Idols and **The Anti-Christ**
Friedrich Schiller	**The Robbers** and **Wallenstein**
Arthur Schopenhauer	**Essays and Aphorisms**
Gottfried von Strassburg	**Tristan**
August Strindberg	**Inferno** and **From an Occult Diary**